The publisher of this book is generously donating all royalties from the retail sales of **REMARKABLE RETIREMENT"** to:

LEMONADE DAY

America was built on the back of small business. Entrepreneurs take risks believing they can realize their dream if they work hard, take responsibility and act as good stewards of their resources. Today's youth share that optimism, but lack the life skills, mentorship and real-world experience necessary to be successful. In 2007, founder Michael Holthouse had a vision to empower today's youth to become tomorrow's entrepreneurs through helping them start, own and operate their very own business...a lemonade stand.

Lemonade Day is a strategic 14-step process that walks youth from a dream to a business plan, while teaching them the same principles required to start any big company. Inspiring kids to work hard and make a profit, they are also taught to spend some, save some and share some by giving back to their community. Since its launch in 2007 in Houston Texas, Lemonade Day has grown from serving 2,700 kids in one city to 1 million children across North America. With the help of partners like Google for Entrepreneurs, Lemonade Day will continue to spark the spirit of entrepreneurship and empower youth to set goals, work hard, and achieve their dreams.

You can learn more about Lemonade Day by visiting:

www.LemonadeDay.org

REMARKABLE RETIREMENT

Conversations with Leading Retirement Experts and Financial Advisors

By Remarkable Press™

Remarkable Retirement/ Mark Imperial. —1st ed.

Managing Editor/ Stewart Andrew Alexander

ISBN-13: 978-0-9987085-4-6

CONTENTS

A NOTE TO THE READER

Thank you for buying your copy of "Remarkable Retirement: Conversations With Leading Retirement Experts and Financial Advisors." This book was originally created as a series of live interviews, that's why it reads like a series of conversations, rather than a traditional book that talks *at you.*

I wanted you to feel as though the participants are talking *with you,* much like a close friend. Creating the material this makes it easier for you to grasp the topics and put them to use quickly, rather than wading through hundreds of pages.

So grab a pen, take notes and get ready to learn some fascinating insights from real world retirement experts.

Warmest regards,

Mark Imperial
Author and Radio Personality

INTRODUCTION

"**Remarkable Retirement: Conversations With Leading Retirement Experts and Financial Advisors**" is a collaborative book series featuring 15 leading Professionals from across the country who are passionate about helping people considering life after retiremnent.

Remarkable Press™ would like to extend a heartfelt thank you to all participants who took the time to submit their chapter and offer their support in becoming *'Get the word out Ambassadors'* for this project.

Remarkable Press™ has pledged 100% of the royalties from the retail sales of this book to be donated to Lemonade Day.

Should you want to make a direct donation, visit their website at: www.LemonadeDay.org

STEVE LEWIT, MA, MRFC

Financial Advisor,
President, Co-Founder, SGL Financial

Email: **slewit@sglfinancial.com**

Website: **www.sglfinancial.com**

Call: **(847) 499-3330**

With 30 years of financial planning and investment advising experience, Steve Lewit deeply understands how important it is for those who are planning their retirement to have a trusted person from whom they can get their financial advice. Steve believes, above all, that there must be a deep trust bond between him and his clients, especially in light of the current financially complex and volatile world.

When you read Steve's many published quotes and articles, such as in the Wall Street Journal, Fox News, Fortune Magazine, Investment News, Chicago Tribune, to name a few, trust, integrity, and the delivery of fiduciary level advice for all are always the central theme. In his most recent book, The Perpetual Retirement Income Machine (Amazon), he explores the latest retirement income strategies and shows you how to maximize income, lower risk, and preserve a higher level of assets for the future by employing the latest research, a holistic approach and an unbiased, creative use of a wide variety of investment and insurance products.

Steve's ultimate goal is to be a financial ally, the person who joins you on your journey through life, and the person from whom you can get your financial questions answered clearly, honestly and objectively about virtually any financial situation.

What kind of clients do you help, and what situations do they find themselves in when they come to you for your help?

There comes a time in each person's life when the 'R' word begins to circulate through their thinking. The 'R' word is, of course, Retirement. Many of my clients discover ongoing thoughts about retirement in their early or mid-forties. At that time, it's a word that just gnaws at them, something that needs attention; for others, especially as they approach closer to retirement, the 'R' word hits them over the head like a jackhammer. These folks are usually older, have saved in their 401k, but have done little else to plan their finances for this most important part of their lives - retirement - when salaries ended, and income must be created through the assets saved during their working years.

When the 'R' word hits, people begin to search for advice. They find that there's plenty available - books to read, financial gurus on the radio and TV, pundit newsletters and, of course, Google. They also find that the quantity of information available is overwhelming; and to make matters more difficult, it is typically conflicting information, with thousands of disparate pieces of advice and commentary, few of which agrees with the other, delivered in microseconds at the push of a button.

When people finally come and meet with me, they are concerned whether they will have enough for retirement, but quite confused about which financial strategies to use. Moreover, having gotten poor advice from advisors in the past, many are distrustful and doubtful that my suggestions and guidance is in their best interests. While money is important, of course, the bigger question for most people is who to trust, and can they trust me? Trust is the core issue for each person I meet, and how to earn that trust is the biggest challenge I have.

What obstacles prevent your clients from achieving their desired outcome?

Mark and Julie, now clients of mine, were 55 years old when I first met them. While every person is uniquely different in how they approach their finances - their risk style, attitudes towards money, biases towards certain products, and their willingness to be coached - Mark and Julie were typical in that they came to me with these three questions:

1. Will our money last as long as we do?

2. How can we get the greatest amount of income at the lowest risk?

3. Why should we trust you?

When I asked them what they have done in the past to get answers to these questions, their answer was remarkably consistent with what most all my clients told me at the beginning of our relationship. They had done a good deal of research on Google; that they had visited a few other advisors; and that they were confused because everything and everybody had a different idea for them. Moreover, and more importantly, they were afraid; afraid of making a mistake regarding the biggest financial decision of their lives, a decision that would dictate the quality of their next 20 - 30 years of life. Their lack of confidence about their finances and their fear of the future was palpable. Fear of the unknown, and how it will turn out, is one of the most difficult emotions to deal with; and that same fear has a deep impact on how and why financial decisions are made (or not made).

Where does that fear come from? What is its effect on health and quality of life? Can it be reduced or even eliminated? These are the deeper questions that I must address with all my clients. Knowing that fear of the future exists at some level for every person, my job as a financial advisor and planner expands far beyond money. Whatever we do must, yes, produce financial results. But it must also produce emotional results, a reduction or elimination of fear along with an enhanced level of confidence and peace of mind.

It is this fear - the fear of not having enough, of suffering in the future, of making a bad decision, of looking stupid, of being taken advantage of, or losing. That stops people in their tracks, blocks trust between advisor and clients, and freezes decision-making, resulting in a continuation of money management that is not in their best interests. Fear closes people off, shuts them down from good advice, and creates the future of which they are afraid. Fear creates a self-fulfilling prophecy, and it is the single greatest obstacle preventing change for the better. If Mark and Julie can't get beyond their fear, their questions will never be answered, and the likelihood of a mediocre or failing retirement dramatically rises.

How have you helped past clients to trust that you were placing their interests over and above your own interests?

Mutual trust enhances honest communication. Candidly, when most shoppers for financial advice first sit in front of a financial advisor, there is very little trust and lots of fear. Typically, neither advisor nor prospective client is aware of how deep the mistrust goes. And that mistrust is well deserved. The sad fact is that while most advisors will claim they are out for the best interests of the client, hidden behind that facade is a desperate need to make a sale. This mistrust undermines - the buyer believing the advisor is nothing more than a salesperson, out for him or herself; the advisor believing that the client will take his or her information, and time, and, after multiple meeting, tell him they need to 'think about it', never to be heard from again.

When Mark and Julie reached the point of believing and trusting that I wasn't out to 'sell' them anything and that I was a true Fiduciary (a Fiduciary is a person who is legally charged to put the interests of the client first, over and above their own interests), they shared with me how many times they have been 'burned' by a financial advisor in the past, and how hard it was to begin to trust that anyone in my industry would truly have their best interests at heart.

Is there a way that Mark and Julie could have avoided learning the hard way about their financial advisors in the past? While nothing is perfect, there are steps to take and things to look for which will minimize the possibility that the advisor is a wolf in sheep's clothing.

Here are three key starter questions to ask any advisor, along with, what I consider, to be satisfactory answers.

1. Are you a Fiduciary, and if I work with you, do we sign an agreement that you are holding yourself out to me as a Fiduciary in our relationship?

   Someone who holds themselves out as a Fiduciary, and signs an agreement with you to that effect, is a necessary condition for which you should insist. Insurance and stockbrokers cannot be Fiduciaries; financial advisors are fiduciaries by definition, but many don't sign an agreement that that is the relationship they have with you. If they don't sign an agreement, their Fiduciary responsibilities are in doubt.

2. Are you objective and unbiased in your choice of products?

    Insurance agents want to sell you insurance products, i.e., Fixed Index Annuities; advisors who specialize in investment in the market, want to solve all your problems with products that carry the risk of loss through the use of mutual funds or stocks and bonds. Unbiased advisors will use any product or a combination of products, market-based or insurance based, as long as that product meets your needs. If an advisor has a bias towards any product or class of products, chances are they are going to push you in that direction over other choices you might have. As soon as you feel the 'push,' it's time to find another advisor.

3. Are you a holistic advisor?

    A well-constructed financial plan includes much more than investments. What about inflation eating up the value of your money; rising healthcare costs, and more especially long-term care costs? Is your estate in order so that your assets pass efficiently to your kids? Are taxes being minimized? Do you qualify for strategies that create tax-free income? Who will counsel you if mom or dad need assisted living, or if your partner or husband has a stroke and can no longer work? Focusing on investments, without considering the whole picture, the holistic picture, is like buying tires for a car but not knowing what make or model. The tires might be great, but they won't fit.

There are more questions to be asked. However, if an advisor answers these questions to your satisfaction, you are off to a great start. On the other hand, unsatisfactory answers are a sure-fire sign that you should head for the door.

What are some of your clients' biggest misconceptions surrounding the topic of finances and managing money?

Okay. Let's say you have found an advisor that meets your qualifications, you have begun to have some trust in that person, and you have begun working together. The next challenge facing your, and the advisor, may surprise you because that challenge is you!

Why?

You come to the table with years and years of theories, opinions, and beliefs about finances, how to manage money, and what you need to do to plan for the future. These theories, opinions, and beliefs have been reinforced by teachers, parents, reading, TV, radio, your research and common conversations with friends and relatives. While some are accurate, many are not; they are just misconceptions that have been reinforced over the years that you have come to believe are true.

It might be something as simple as Mark and Julie having a very negative attitude towards the stock market because Mom and Dad lost a bundle in the market and told them, over and over again, how stupid they thought they were, and hope that their children didn't make the same stupid mistake. Or it could be another client's opinion that all annuities were laden with expenses; or that the world is ending and you should buy gold; or that you should never pay a fee to have your money managed.

We all know that old habits and beliefs are hard to discard. An advisor who is a Fiduciary, holistic, unbiased, and objective can give you the greatest advice, but if you hold on to the old messages circulating in your head, that advice may go for naught. In other words, you may trust in that advisor but have so many fixed misconceptions, that nothing gets done.

What to do?

A good advisor will approach you with an open mind. He or she will ask a lot of questions to see the world through your eyes, so he can understand you better and, therefore, advise you better. That's his job.

Your job is to be candid with the advisor about what you're thinking and why you think the way you do about money. Upon hearing your concerns or points of view, a well-trained advisor will provide concrete evidence - research, data, articles, etc.- to help you understand the difference between reality and your misconceptions. It's then your job to let go of the old mistruths and embrace the reality of your advisor's advice. On the other hand, if the advisor loses patience, or doesn't present you with research based on objective evidence, then you need to either insist on that evidence or find another advisor who can help you understand yourself and the financial industry's point of view in a better and healthier way.

At the same time, you don't want to naively take the advice of your advisor without question or discussion. I have two rules in my practice which are very important to my clients and, I believe, to you too:

Rule #1: If you don't fully understand something, you don't do it!

Rule #2: If whatever you're thinking of doing doesn't give you greater peace of mind, you don't do it!

If your advisor doesn't think that way, make sure you do!

What pitfalls or mistakes should people considering their retirement options keep in mind?

I remember the moment when Mark and Julie asked me a question I had heard many times in the past. Theirs was, however, phrased more succinctly, and right-on, "Steve, how can we be savvier about our money and your industry? How can we separate the truth from the BS?"

I had thought about that question and how to answer it for a long time before they asked. The problem is that there are so many layers to the financial industry and the products offered, so many places a person could be misled, misrepresented, lied to, exaggerated to, or outright frauded. It seemed to me that if someone wanted to be savvy about my industry they would need to have all the experiences and training that I have. And, even with the level of savvy I have, stuff comes up for me which is new and off the charts all the time. Mine is a very complex, quickly changing, often devious industry.

I explained to Mark and Julie, as I now explain to all my clients, everything has pros and cons. If an advisor is presenting only the pros, that advisor is trying to sell you something, not being square with you, not truly educating you. To become savvy about money, you need to associate yourself with those who are savvy and, at the same time, willing to open the windows and look into this hidden and often deceptive world.

Your advisor should make you aware, more aware than you already are, about things you don't know or think you know. That advisor will show you:

- How to read between the lines of misleading advertising

- How to find the hidden fees

- How to sniff out what a Ponzi scheme looks and sounds like

- How to determine if rates of returns promised by investment managers that are much too high

- What the ulterior motive of the person presenting to you or trying to get you to buy something is, i.e., to get good television ratings or to sell you a book for example.

To become savvy about money is to wake up and be alert to all the possibilities; not to be blinded by promises that sound good and make you feel good; to be honest and real with yourself, and to make sure that the advisor you are working with is honest and real with you.

What are some of your client's most common fears about managing their finances?

If managing finances and creating solid financial plans were easy, advisors and financial planners would go out of business. As we've seen, planning a retirement that may last 20 - 30 years in a volatile economic, market and financial atmosphere, hand in hand with the fears, misconceptions, biases that you, the consumer, bring to the table, in an industry that remains hidden and non-transparent, with advisors that are not objective and biased, not know what you don't know, and having little confidence in what you do know, can be a daunting task. The fact is that this is a complex subject, at a complex time, where you have to make decisions that will affect the rest of your life. It is not easy; and if you think it is, think again.

Based on all that, I often wonder why everyone doesn't have a Fiduciary level, holistic adviser. What holds them back? Is it the fear of failure, of making a big mistake, having so much mistrust they'd rather be their own advisors? Is it their reticence for paying a fee, of being duped, or looking dumb? While I believe that all these fears are percolating in the background, I also believe the real reason people don't hire a holistic, unbiased, fiduciary level advisor, is that they simply don't the value that a trusted advisor will add to their financial management, confidence, and peace of mind, or they don't know where to find one?

Mark and Julie, when they first came to me had another advisor who they did like, for over seven years. They talked to this person about two times a year; their growth rate was acceptable, and they thought they were getting the best of what the financial industry had to offer.

During our first conversation, I asked, as I tend to do, some questions. Here are just a few and, as you will see, are very telling:

1. When you told your advisor that you were thinking about retirement and wanted to make sure you have all your ducks in order, he gave you a written retirement income plan. Did you bring it with you?

   Answer: He never gave us a written plan.

2. When you and your advisor discussed the growth goal for your portfolio, what rate did you agree on?

   Answer: Oh, I think we are trying to do the best we can do.

3. When you and your advisor discussed how much your portfolio could lose in a down market like 2008, what did he tell you?

   Answer: We never discussed losses, only gains.

4. When you and your advisor discussed your options for using market vs. insurance products how did you determine that most all your money belongs in the market?

   Answer: We never discussed insurance products?

5. I can see here that you have chosen not to plan any tax-free retirement income for the future. Is there a reason you passed on that?

Answer: I didn't know you could get tax-free retirement income.

What is the value of peace of mind? What is the value of knowing that you have someone in your corner that advocates first and foremost, for you? What is the value of knowing you will be okay in the future?

Every price or fee has a corresponding value. If the value isn't there, the fee is not worth paying. Many people are too focused on the fee, rather than the value. A Fiduciary level advisor, one who is not biased towards certain products or strategies, and who truly has your best interests at heart, can have tremendous value for you, a value on which you cannot put a price. Mark and Julie, and all my clients have discovered the retirement journey requires much more than someone managing your money in the stock market, or the purchase of a few annuities that some insurance agent sold to you. Remember, it's never about the money, it's always about the quality of your life.

It sounds obvious, but why would the people you serve want to achieve this outcome?

I've talked a lot about gaining peace of mind around your finances, that life isn't always about money, and that money is just fuel for your journey. But, what exactly is peace of mind, and why is it so important?

After doing a lot of research, mostly psychological and behavioral, about peace of mind, it became clear to me that research verifies what we all know, that most human beings have a fear of the unknown, and the future is always unknown.

In my discussions with Mark and Julie, it became clear that Julie's fear of the future was far greater than Mark's. She had very little peace of mind about money; while Mark, while not comfortable at all, felt good about their future and didn't lose any sleep over it. Mark was at a much higher level of peace of mind than Julie. While their marriage was solid, they were not on the same page when it came to their finances.

Moreover, Mark as it turned out, was a short-term thinker; and Julie thought far out into the future. Mark perceived his life on what would happen in two to three months; Julie perceived her life on what would happen 10 to 20 years from now. Not surprisingly, some of their conversation over their finances were not pleasant.

Peace of mind is an individual affair, i.e., Mark's peace of mind vs. Julie's peace of mind. But then there's the peace of mind of Mark and Julie as a couple, as partners. That's an extra layer which few people consider and which, knowingly or not, a layer which deeply impacts the quality of any relationship. While we all think we understand peace of mind, our desire for it, and its effect on us as individuals and couples, few have thought about what it is, how it works, and how it is best gained, especially when it comes to money.

Many people have shared with me that when they sit with a financial advisor the more important conversation is not about their money, but it's about how their money can give them confidence and peace of mind about the future. Instead of focusing on numbers, they want the advisor to help them understand much more than percentages and growth rates, but how those figures affect them emotionally, especially when it comes to meeting their ultimate goal of knowing that their finances will serve them well for the next 20 - 30 years of retirement.

Peace of mind stems from a deeply rooted confidence that you know that whatever happens, you will be okay. People that have well-developed retirement income plans, along with an advisor who has joined them at the hip on their journey, create a rock solid financial foundation for their future. It is a foundation built on research, logic, understanding, and trust. It is not a foundation of shifting sand, purchasing a product here and there, and getting advice from this or that person impulsively. When there is clear sailing ahead, things run smoothly. And, when the ill winds come, as sure as they will, those winds can be managed wisely, without fear of ending up on the rocks. Peace of mind is the most powerful emotion available to humans. It is hard to gain and easy to lose. Most people ride peace of mind like a roller coaster, feeling good when the market is up, and miserable when the market is down. Life doesn't have to be that way when it comes to your money. Money can be made to work like a machine where you turn the switch, and it just hums along producing income and confidence for the rest of your life.

What led you to this field?

Like you, and all my clients, I strive for peace of mind in my life too. My past is filled with the search to find that secret ingredient, the one that will give me more than a temporary moment of fulfillment and peace of mind, only to shift to stress or unrest when things change. Early on in my life, I realized that from a work perspective, I needed to follow my passion, and if I didn't, peace of mind was out of my reach. So, I did. And those passions first led me to play professional tennis; then to become a professional opera singer; and finally, my deepest passion became known, my passion for guiding people on their financial journey through life. Perhaps my background as an economist - I have an MA in economics and taught economics at the college level - turned me to money and finances, which flowered with me becoming a financial advisor.

If you asked me what I bring to the table as an advisor, why I am different, why you should work with me, the answer is singular - I am extremely passionate about what I do. And, that passion drives me to higher levels of achievement so I can better serve those with whom I work. While perfection cannot be reached, when it comes to planning and care for my clients, my aim to be perfect cannot be daunted or gainsaid.

Unknown to Mark and Julie when they first came to visit with me, I understood that one of my goals was to help them find their passion, and then provide the economic and financial basis upon which they could fulfill it. This is what I mean when I say that life isn't about the money; it's about life.

I have found, and probably you have found, that people who are living their passion are full of life; they are energetic, older in age but young in their thinking; they are happy; confident; and can't wait to get up in the morning to begin their day. To me, this is what money is all about. It is much more important than what next year's growth rate may be; which stock to buy or sell; or what the fee is (note that I'm not saying those things are unimportant, but they mean little in comparison to being given financial freedom so that you can live your passion).

What are your final thoughts?

Remarkable retirements begin with remarkable people. In my view, each person I meet is remarkable - they have remarkable stories, and all have done remarkable things in their lives. Some of my clients think they are just ordinary people. They are not. To me, each person is a partially discovered treasure with an immense treasure chest in the background just waiting to be fully opened. The release of that treasure through the elements of well-managed finances is what my passion and my practice are all about.

Is it possible to do it yourself?

Of course.

Is it possible for you to succeed through all the years ahead of you?

Absolutely.

Is it possible for you to find confidence and peace of mind without any outside guidance?

Sure.

The question is, is that the best route for you or is there a better, more efficient way to solve the retirement puzzle.

Mark and Julie told me a story about their experience in thinking about retirement. They shared that it was one night, fairly late in the evening, the house was quiet, and they were sipping a glass of wine together. It was, they said, one of those rare times when both were relaxed, and they felt truly connected. The conversation was easy, open, and clear. When the conversation eased into the topic of their eventual retirement, both shared with each other the stress and uncertainty that began to rise within them.

A half-hour later that uncertainty turned into fear that they didn't know whether their retirement would be a financially healthy retirement or one filled with stress, arguments, and a lifestyle below their standard. That conversation was the singular reason they came to see me and became my clients - the relief of having a holistic plan, a Fiduciary on their side, and the peace of mind of being able to move forward, into the unknown, with confidence that all will turn around right.

Your story is a story I would love to hear. And, making your story a great story in the future, is something I would love to do with you. Financial advice is easily available to you from what seems like an infinite number of sources. Holistic, objective, unbiased and comprehensive financial advice is, unfortunately, hard to find. Like you, I can't foresee the future and what it will bring. Because of that, I welcome a meeting with anyone who is interested in improving the finances and quality of life. I have no minimums, no requirements, and no planning fees. The only requirement to work with me is an open mind, the willingness to be honest, and a sincere desire to do much better in the future.

If the reader wants to know more, what's the easiest way to find you?

I invite you to get a copy of my new book, The Perpetual Retirement Income Machine (Amazon) and visit my website - www.sglfinancial.com - to learn more about my team and me. It would be my pleasure to have a conversation with you to explore your future and see if it makes sense for me to be a financial ally on your journey.

GABRIEL LEWIT

CEO & Co-Founder

SGL Financial

Email: **glewit@SGLfinancial.com**
Website: **www.SGLfinancial.com**
LinkedIn: **www.linkedin.com/in/lewitgd**
Facebook: **www.facebook.com/lewitgd**
Twitter: **www.twitter.com/lewitgd**
Other: **www.instagram.com/lewitgd**
Call: **(847) 499-3331**

If there is a single word that can describe Gabriel's life journey towards becoming an advisor, it's dedication.

Gabriel has always been dedicated to many different things, like supporting his family, helping others and always doing what's right. It's this dedication combined with hard work and perseverance that's allowed him to accomplish so much so early in his career.

Gabriel and his father, Steve, co-founded SGL Financial together in 2007, and Gabriel's been practicing as a financial advisor for over 11 years. He's passionate about helping his clients achieve their goals through a collaborative, comprehensive and holistic financial planning approach.

More importantly, Gabriel is dedicated to ensuring his clients' success – both personal and financial – and to building meaningful, trusting and enduring relationships together.

Outside of work, you'll find Gabriel spending time with his wife Dede, his son Nathan, his daughter Audrey and their three hyperactive dogs (all Doodles!). He's an ambitious entrepreneur, an avid Chicago Sports fan and he loves traveling, soccer, technology, friends and eating great food. Be sure to ask him what his favorite meal is!

Describe the clients you work with and the types of situations they find themselves in when they come to you for your help?

What's unique about our approach at SGL Financial is that we've specifically built our firm to ensure we can help every type of client who walks through our doors.

Some clients have asked us if that means we're generalists, and the answer is an emphatic *no*. Instead, we've structured our firm by building an expansive team of advisors and specialists who, collectively, provide us the requisite experience and expertise needed to work with everyone in any situation

As one of the founders of SGL Financial, I personally love this approach because it's been our mission from day one to provide financial service and support to anyone who needs it. We don't have hefty minimums, we don't serve just the rich, and we don't turn people away who need our help just because they don't have a lot of money.

Unless someone has absolutely no money at all to invest, there is always something we can do to help them build wealth, improve their finances, their personal well-being, and their overall life satisfaction.

With that in mind, our typical client is searching for a firm that's a one-stop-shop. They are seeking a relationship with a financial advisor they can feel confident in, they can trust, and they can rely on for every financial need they have.

The most common situations our clients have with their finances depend on what stage of life they're in.

For our younger clients or clients with growing families, it's about establishing a solid financial plan, providing life insurance protection for their loved ones, and beginning to ramp up their retirement savings.

For our clients who are nearing retirement or in retirement, it's always about generating income and preserving assets. With ever-increasing life expectancies, it's more critical than ever to have an income plan in place to support your lifestyle.

We specialize in helping our retirement-age clients build a "Perpetual Retirement Income Machine" that they can never outlive, and which helps preserve their assets, so they never run out of money.

Lastly, we offer specialty services for a variety of other types of clients, including business owners, entrepreneurs, health-care professionals, teachers, and federal employees.

No matter what financial circumstances you find yourself in, we hope you feel confident that the team we've built at SGL Financial has the knowledge and experience you're looking for.

What common obstacles prevent your clients from seeking a financial advisor relationship they can feel confident in?

For many of my personal clients, the biggest challenge they encounter is fear, worry, and doubt, and this can manifest itself in a variety of ways.

When some of my clients needed help, they worried they didn't have enough money and that an advisor wouldn't want to spend any time with them, so they initially didn't come in for an appointment.

If that's a fear for you too, please put that fear to rest and remember that we don't have strict minimums and we pride ourselves in our ability to help as many types of clients as possible.

For our younger clients who are raising kids or putting money away for college, the fear tends to revolve around saving for retirement, even if that retirement date is decades away.

Think about it this way. When all your money is being spent on your children and family, the underlying fear is, "How do I save for myself" and "If I can't save for myself, how will I retire one day?" So, while it's not always easy to spot, retirement worries are a big cause of financial stress even for the younger clients we meet with.

For our retirement-age clients, either nearing retirement or in retirement, the question and the fear turns more concretely to "how do I avoid running out of money?"

There are studies that show that the majority of people fear running out of money even more than they fear death.

The reason for this is that psychologically speaking, security of one's basic needs such as food, shelter, and safety are paramount to one's ability to feel secure in life and to be able to enjoy everything else that life has to offer. Without enough income, our basic needs such as food, shelter, and safety can feel at risk.

A big component of our practice is helping create a guaranteed 'income floor' for our retirement age clients. This guaranteed income then covers all of their essential living expenses.

These clients of ours sleep confidently knowing all of their key retirement costs are covered, and their income will never go down due to any economic downturns or market drops and collapses.

By approaching planning this way, it frees our clients from any worry and doubt, leaving them focused on what opportunities they can enjoy in their retirement!

Another common concern for investors is knowing who to trust.

Many of our clients have worked with a variety of financial planners and advisers throughout their lives. For the most part, many financial firms and advisers really care about their clients and do a great job, but there are, as always, bad apples in the mix that can sometimes tarnish the industry's reputation and give other advisors a bad name.

Unfortunately, many people that have been burned in the past, or who have received average service and advice, fear change more than they fear the consequences of just keeping things the same.

As a result, they don't realize that a truly *great advisor* may be waiting out there and they decide to just live with the status quo instead.

What we would like to tell these clients is don't stop searching for that A + advisor or financial firm. They are out there. You *can* find an advisor that you can connect with, that you can call for any question big or small. An advisor you know will be there for you and who will always put your best interests first. You just have to keep looking until you find them!

Our firm, as a Registered Investment Adviser, is held legally to a Fiduciary Standard, meaning we must always put our clients' interests first ahead of our own.

Many of our clients don't know this, but a majority of the financial professionals in the industry are *not* held to this Fiduciary Standard, and can sometimes provide solutions that are only OK for the client, but better for them or their firm.

Trust, of course, is something that is built over time, but it starts with the right foundation of honesty, forthrightness, communication, and respect. We know that you'll experience all of these things when working with SGL Financial, so we hope you don't settle for anything less.

One other obstacle to financial success we see is procrastination. Let's face it, we all procrastinate in life. In fact, for many people, it's one of their favorite things to do. Why do today what we can put off tomorrow, right? *Just kidding!*

The reality is, we don't mean to procrastinate on purpose, but we all do it because life can just be so darn busy sometimes.

We are often juggling ten, fifteen, twenty things at a time on our personal to-do lists, not to mention work, family, friends or the never-ending list of chores and errands we need to run on a weekly and monthly basis.

When it comes to your finances, however, there are a few key things to consider regarding procrastination and how it impacts your life.

The first is, the '*no-plan*' plan is not a plan at all. If you are just winging it with your finances, or haven't really gotten a completed plan together, your chances of reaching your ideal financial destination aren't very good.

Think of it like taking a cross-country road trip from New York to California. You'd map out your route, plan your hotel stops, pack a few changes of clothes, bring some snacks, charge your phone, grab your wallet, and gas up your car. That way you know you're all set for the journey ahead and will successfully reach your destination in an efficient manner.

Well, imagine if you just woke up tomorrow morning at 7:30 AM, threw on some flip-flops and just jumped in the car without any maps, phone or navigation system and just started driving. Something tells me those two trips won't look alike!

So, is your financial plan really in place and does it cover everything it needs to for your retirement planning journey?

The second thing to consider is that procrastination can potentially cost you a lot of money.

For every week, month, or year you aren't invested in the right portfolio, or your 'no-plan' plan is taking you in the wrong direction, you could be losing money either by taking far too much risk than you should be in the market, by vastly underperforming with your portfolio, or in many cases, both taking too much risk and underperforming.

The technical term for this is 'opportunity cost' and it can really add up.

By finding the right advisor and the right team to work with, you'll have confidence that your plan is designed the right way to strategically keep you on the right financial path. No more lost opportunity cost for you!

Third, and most importantly, by *not* procrastinating (i.e., taking action) and getting everything in place, you gain much greater peace-of-mind and clarity.

There's no more thinking about this hanging over your shoulder. You don't have to wonder what your retirement plan will look like anymore, or worry about if you'll run out of money.

People often underestimate how much these financial worries they tuck in the back of their mind really impact them. So, what we suggest is that you *un-tuck them* from the back of your mind, bring them to the front, and take action on them by scheduling an appointment with an advisor, whether or not that's with us at SGL Financial.

Either way, it's just important to do it.

The 'worst' thing that happens by meeting with an advisor for a check-up is that you learn what you're doing now is great and you don't need to change. The best thing that happens is you gain strategies, insights, and actionable items you can take to better your financial future and increase your peace-of-mind.

How have you helped past clients to overcome obstacles and gain direction, confidence, and peace-of-mind?

I'd like to give one example of a client-case that we worked on that really helps illustrate how we help our clients gain direction, confidence, and peace-of-mind.

Mary *(Name has been changed for Privacy Purposes)* was 58 years old and has worked as a chef and part-time caterer for most of her career, providing meals to children at local schools or other venues.

Mary, for most of her life, had used a family recommendation for a tax-preparer to do her taxes each year. She had never had a huge amount of investable assets, only about $200,000 saved, so she thought that most advisors wouldn't want to work with her. She just managed her assets on her own, and they weren't performing too well.

Soon, the relationship with her tax-preparer started to deteriorate, and Mary chose to work with SGL Financial to do her taxes.

After completing her return, she realized it made sense to have us take a look at her finances, and asked if she could schedule an appointment and financial check-up. She had a number of unanswered questions and didn't really know who to talk to about them.

As for her $200,000 of assets, Mary had a few 401(k) accounts from previous employers that were just sitting idle and wanted to know what to do with them. Her house was completely paid off, which she was quite proud of. However, she didn't have a specific plan in place for when she wanted to retire, although she was starting to think about retiring in about 10 years if it were financially possible.

While it hadn't been a top priority for her previously, she realized that if retirement was potentially just 10 years away, she wanted to know what to do with her money so she could get to her retirement date with confidence.

After working with SGL to develop a retirement income plan, Mary implemented her plan which had a component to guarantee her retirement income at age 65 and a component to invest her 401(k) IRA rollover money in a portfolio that was a good match for her risk-personality, but one that could also generate a good rate of return.

Mary also learned that she didn't need to have lots of money to retire and was able to gain clarity and confidence in her plan utilizing the assets that she had available. Even more exciting to her, her plan showed she would be able to retire in only 7 or 8 years instead of the 10 years she was initially expecting!

Share some of the common misconceptions that your clients may have about achieving their financial and retirement goals.

Something I see frequently is clients of ours - *before they come in to meet with u*s - believe that building a financial plan is overwhelming, complex and a lot of work to create.

We sometimes cringe when we see our clients come to us with a financial plan from one of our competitors, or from one of the big-box financial institutions.

Some of these plans are 75-125 pages or longer, and most clients don't have a clue what's in them or what they say or mean. They *just* sit on a shelf and gather dust. This doesn't serve anyone any good.

At SGL Financial, our process results in a simple, easy-to-understand, 1-page overview and summary of your financial and retirement plan. Yes, really, 1-page!

Sure, there are some additional reports and details supporting that summary, but you'll *never* get a huge stack of papers with tons of graphs and charts yet not a clue what your plan actually is. We strive to ensure that creating a plan with us is simple, straightforward and dare we even say 'fun' for a number of our clients.

Something else we've heard from our clients is that they thought our free financial check-up process was not really free, or that there is some sort of catch, or that there would be pressure to make a purchase or decision of some kind.

When these clients did decide to meet with us, we took the time to explain our process, our approach, how we work and what makes us different.

They learned that our free check-up really doesn't cost a thing, there is no catch, and it really is 100% pressure free. The only decision you have to make at the end of it is whether or not it makes sense to meet again to keep the conversation going.

The best way to describe the first meeting with us, or a free check-up meeting with us, is that it's really just a conversation. We want to get a chance to get to know you - your goals, your dreams, your concerns - and give you the opportunity to know us - our personalities, our approach, what makes us unique.

That's the best foundation for a future relationship together!

What unknown pitfalls should the reader be aware of?

A big area to watch out for with your finances are the hidden costs of taxes. When we begin to review a client's current financial plan and current portfolio, we're going to take a big look at tax-efficiency. Too many advisors ignore tax-efficiency planning when they build a financial plan for their clients.

Sure, they focus on income planning, asset allocation, and investment portfolio selection. But that's not going far enough.

Remember, it's not about what percentage return you earn, or how much you make, it's about how much you keep *net-after-taxes*. The more tax-efficient you are, the more you make.

Our unique approach specializes in being tax-efficient or even tax-free whenever possible, utilizing a combination of methods to help reduce your tax burden both today but also in the future when tax rates are unknown and could be much higher than they are today.

Another mistake we see is not knowing how much risk you are taking in your current investment portfolio. All too often, our clients can't tell us what they have in their portfolio or why they even have it in the first place.

The typical reason is simply *"that's just what our advisor recommended."*

Moreover, when we ask how much risk they are taking, and how much their portfolio might lose in the next market crash or correction, people simply have no idea!

A well-designed investment portfolio, which is one key component of a well-designed financial plan, should have a clearly defined investment methodology that you can understand.

That means you know exactly <u>what</u> is in your portfolio, <u>why</u> it's there, and <u>how</u> to expect it to perform. More importantly, you also know how to <u>protect</u> and <u>secure</u> your portfolio and nest-egg.

At SGL Financial you'll always have an Investment Policy Statement that helps you define risk and return expectations for your portfolio so that you know it's the right one for you based on your personal market risk tolerance and your personal goals.

What are your clients' biggest fears surrounding income planning?

Some of our clients worry that working with us will be too expensive. One of the things we pride ourselves most on at SGL Financial is that we are fee transparent and we have structured our firm to be able to help people of all types and in all stages of their lives.

In your first meeting or your free financial check-up with us, we'll absolutely discuss any fees associated with working together. We have different solutions and different ways of working with clients that have different fee structures or even no fees at all.

We're confident that you won't find it too expensive to work with us!

It's also typical for clients to worry about meeting minimum investment requirements when working with a new advisor. SGL Financial is unique in that we don't have any minimums.

We have built our company specifically to be able to help clients that have smaller account sizes, medium account sizes, larger account sizes and also ultra-high-net-worth individuals and families.

More importantly, we give everybody the same high level of service, attention, and support, regardless of account size!

Lastly, it's also common to think that retirement income planning is too time-consuming. Our clients think it will take too much time to get a plan in place and that they won't have enough time to commit to the process.

Of course, it takes a time-commitment from both sides to get your financial plan initially started, but instead of thinking of planning as a one-time-event, think of it as an ongoing journey of lifelong financial maintenance and support, and that we are here for you whenever you need us.

A common misconception is that we have a giant checklist and we have to get everything done all at once to complete your plan. However, that's not the case. It's usually too overwhelming for both us and for you.

Instead, we focus on the top priority of your plan and work on that first. Once we get that done, we can move on to the next item. As time evolves, your plan, needs, goals, and concerns will evolve too, and we'll simply revisit any areas that we need to adjust and revise accordingly.

No matter how busy your schedule, there are always ways to streamline our meeting process, whether it's meeting by phone, Skype, lunch appointments or otherwise.

We know how important and how scarce time is, and we'll work with you accordingly to ensure we make progress on your financial planning and also respect your time commitments.

It sounds obvious, but why would the people you serve want to work with financial advisors they feel they can trust and help them to achieve financial freedom?

Our guiding mission at SGL Financial is *Building Wealth for Life.* In our minds, this means two things.

First, financial planning and wealth management is a lifelong journey, not a one-time event. Our team of advisors and support personnel and here to help support and guide you as you build wealth your entire life. No matter what phase of life you're in, we're here to help you manage it financially, personally, and emotionally.

Second, when you build wealth, you don't do it just to have more money in your bank account to stare at, you do it to enjoy your *life* with that wealth.

Building wealth is about building financial freedom, and financial freedom allows you to live the life you've always wanted to without worrying about whether or not you have the money to be able to support it.

Our mission at SGL Financial is to serve each and every one of our clients with a deep, meaningful personal relationship and to empower each of our clients to build wealth for their own lives.

Think of us as *your ally* on your financial journey. We're here for you at your side, when you need us, always.

In taking this approach, we can empower clients who feel happy, secure and who can live their lives without worrying about money all the time. They know that we're here for them for *any* question of *any* kind, that we've got their back, and that we're watching over their money and their finances right alongside with them.

Our clients are ready to stop worrying about their money and ready to start living their life knowing that their finances are well taken care of.

What led you to the financial services field?

I've always been very passionate about helping people and educating others. As an example, even from a very young age, I'd try to help my friends with their homework at school, giving them answers to hard questions and helping them figure out how to solve them on their own.

At the age of 14, I became a Snowboard Instructor at Okemo Mountain, helping beginners and those looking for advanced help with table-top jumps or the halfpipe. In college at Clarkson University, I became a Computer Science Tutor to help those who found computer programming really difficult (which many people do!)

The reason I chose financial planning, on the other hand, has to do with growing up with my mom and the lessons that she taught me.

At the age of 4, my parents divorced, and I moved to Vermont with my mom, who after the divorce was a single mother raising two young children. She did the best she could, working 50+ hours a week as a School Psychologist for $28,000 a year, as well as working part-time jobs to help provide for my sister and me.

One day when I was in first grade, mom took me to the local bank after school to open my first savings account with a few allowance dollars she had given to me for doing chores. This was her way of teaching me the importance of working to earn money and also the importance of saving it from a very young age.

This was just the start of her teaching me some sound fundamentals of personal finance, although at the time I remember being pretty frustrated that I couldn't use that money to buy candy at the convenience store!

Growing up in rural Vermont (which has very little industry, very few job opportunities, and a challenging economy), we certainly weren't anywhere close to wealthy. In fact, we were pretty poor, but my mom always managed to provide for us with fresh berries for breakfast, healthy school lunches, summer vacations in Maine, stylish clothes, Friday night pizza outings, and more.

As I grew up, I didn't think much of this, but after college, I learned that through all of this, my mom had managed to save upwards of $600,000 dollars towards her retirement by scrimping and saving and investing wisely.

How she accomplished this still amazes me to this day. I've learned a lot from her and her smart financial decisions, and have always wanted to help teach others to make the same.

By combining my passions for helping people, building relationships, educating others, and my experience in personal finance, there is no other field that suits me better than financial planning and wealth management. I hope to be able to share some of that passion for financial improvement with you!

What are your final thoughts for someone wanting to improve either their finances, their lives or both?

I would encourage you to think closely about what type of advisor or firm you are aligning yourself with. Interview a few different advisors and be sure that you choose one that you connect with financially and personally.

You also have to get out there and *do it*, not just put it off for next week, next month or next year.

When you do take that step of finding an advisor, you want to be sure that the firm you choose, and the advisor you select, are philosophically aligned with you in the right key areas:

- Will your advisor be there for you when you need them?

- Will your advisor return your calls promptly?

- Will your advisor listen to your needs, concerns, goals, and fears?

- Will your advisor put your interests first, before their own?

- Will your advisor be your ally on your lifelong financial journey?

There are so many important questions to ask and items to look for when choosing an advisor. Don't be afraid of asking them!

But most importantly, you have to feel confidence, trust and a great personal connection with your advisor and their firm.

I believe strongly that the firm we've built at SGL Financial can help provide you with all of those, and I hope you choose to meet with one of our advisors or me and experience our difference for yourself.

If the reader wants to know more, how can they connect with you?

To learn more about us, please visit our website at www.SGLfinancial.com. We have a lot of terrific educational resources, videos, articles and much more. You can also use the website to request your free financial check-up too. We hope you enjoy learning more about SGL Financial and we really hope to meet with you soon.

BARBARA TRAYLOR SMITH

Financial Professional, Owner
Retirement Outfitters, LLC

Email: **barbara@gjretire.com**

Website: **www.gjretire.com**

LinkedIn: **Barbara Traylor Smith**

Facebook: **Retirement Outfitters, LLC**

Call: **(970) 256-1748**

Barbara Traylor Smith's path to becoming a financial professional began when she received her BA in Accounting from Southwest Texas State University. Following graduation, she worked in public accounting in national and regional firms, earning her CPA designation in 1990.

Then, she served as the primary liaison between advisors and the home office of several insurance companies, in other words she was the advisor's' advisor. Barbara has trained many advisors in all aspects of the retirement & financial planning process including general investments, tax advantaged investments, life and disability insurance, long term care insurance and annuity policies.

Through education and experience gleaned over a career spanning 30+ years, she is well qualified to help her clients plan their retirement utilizing many different tools and techniques. Currently, Barbara is the President of Retirement Outfitters, LLC in Grand Junction, CO & is an Independent Wealth Advisor with WealthSource Partners.

Describe the clients you work with and the types of situations they find themselves in when they come to you for your help?

Most of the people that come to see me are folks who are heading towards retirement and want to make sure that they don't outlive their savings. Their concern is spending too much money in their early retirement on fun things that would create a financial crisis in their later years. They tend to be in their late 50s or early 60s and have saved for retirement but don't necessarily have a plan to *use* their savings in a wise and prudent manner.

For example, Joe and Sue came to see me recently. They were a few years from retirement and live on about $5,000 a month. They are going to receive about $3,000 a month from Social Security and wanted to know how to generate the additional $2,000 a month needed to meet their normal living expenses. You've probably heard over the years that you need to have 80% of your current income to be able to retire, but is that going to be enough?

It didn't sound like enough to them. In fact, most retirees spend more in early retirement than later. We were able to analyze their future income and expenses, accounting for cost of living adjustments, then use our program to show them that they were able to retire, do the things they wanted to do, and be able to provide for themselves in their later years.

What common obstacles prevent your clients from understanding their investments?

I find that many folks get close to retirement and realize that they have saved a pile of money to "secure" their retirement but they don't actually know how to use those savings to ensure the money will last their lifetime. My main goal is to help people overcome this obstacle by gathering information and building a plan that helps them know that they can do the fun things they want to do without jeopardizing their future.

For example, the Williams' have a good stream of guaranteed income for retirement between Social Security benefits, pension income, and other sources, so they do not need to access their retirement assets. Then there are the McMillans, who only have Social Security benefits, so they need to use their retirement assets to provide income. These are two very different scenarios and require very different planning strategies.

When my clients and I are discussing how much financial risk is appropriate for their portfolio, my answer is not what they expect to hear. I want to know how much you spend! We then calculate the income needed from your portfolio to maintain your standard of living. We want our folks to have enough planned income to cover their living expenses. The Have-to-Have expenses. Remember we talked about the Williams earlier? They weren't going to need income from their portfolio. On the other hand, the McMillans were absolutely going to need monthly income from their portfolio. These two situations illustrate how the amount of risk you should take can vary and the asset allocation ratio between no/low-risk products and higher risk products is determined accordingly.

It all depends on how much you have, how much you spend, and how long you're going to live. Well, we don't know the last one of course! So, we plan long because if we plan short, then you'll be coming to me saying...what do I do now?! We want your money to work for you and not the other way around. That is why our motto is, "It's not about your money, it's about your life!"

What misguided truths do your clients have about finances and their retirement?

Whether you are a do-it-yourselfer or not, you may benefit from an advisor guiding you along the way. A recent

Vanguard study suggests that investors could potentially add 3% to their net returns with the help of an advisor.[1] We know that financial acuity decreases for most people over time. Frequently, one spouse is more versed in the financial matters of the household. When that person is no longer able to make the decisions, mistakes can be made, and finances become a stress in their lives. When they have an advisor to lean on they are able to get a second opinion before settling on a decision, the non-financial spouse has someone to go to that has the approval of their spouse.

This was true for Mary and Bob; Bob had always been the decision maker of the finances in their relationship. When Bob was diagnosed with Alzheimer's, he knew that Mary would not be comfortable making all the decisions on her own. We worked together while he was able, to create a plan that would set a path for Mary to follow when he was no longer able to contribute. A plan can create peace of mind, for you, your spouse, and your family.

Also, financial products have changed dramatically in the last 10 or 20 years. They may have the same name, but the offerings today are quite different than those of the past. This

---

[1] According to Vanguard's study based on their Alpha framework. Putting a value on your value: Quantifying Vanguard's Alpha, Vanguard Research, 2014. https://www.vanguard.com/pdf/ISGQVAA.pdf

is probably due to consumer demand and technology changing the way the financial markets operate. For example, it was very common in the past to derive income from bond ladders and dividend stocks. But today, there are many more ways to create income streams that were never available in the past. Folks don't always recognize these differences and make decisions without learning all of their options. An advisor can help identify the options in many areas.

Have you also noticed that there is a massive amount of information on retirement planning available? Whether it's TV, radio, magazines, internet, friends, and family, there's a lot of noise out there. Much of this information is conflicting, wouldn't you agree? What do you do when you get conflicting information? You may be like many people who get confused and then paralyzed, preventing you from making any decisions at all. This could be the worst mistake that some folks will make. An advisor can help you sort through all the information and find that which applies to you.

While there is no guarantee that the advisor you choose will be the perfect one, there are some things you can do to find one that is a good fit for you and your family. It's important to interview an advisor before you make a selection. We offer many opportunities for folks to get to know me. Our group workshops are great since you can see how we interact and begin to understand our philosophy, while my individual meetings help you get all of your personal questions answered. We also have a website, www.GJretire.com, which offers valuable information to stay connected. We believe this is a long-term relationship and you better like us!

If you're like me, thinking about retiring can be exciting! You'll have all the time in the world to do exactly what you want to do. The question is, what are you going to do? Even if you are financially prepared to retire at age 66, doesn't mean you should. In the book, Retire Right, Dr. Fraunfelder & Dr. Gilbaugh identify the 4 phases of retirement and note that those who stay in Phase 2 - Semi-retirement, live the longest and are the happiest.

If you're not financially prepared, keep working! This idea of retirement is only a 130-year-old social experiment which began when Germany adopted the old-age social insurance program in 1889. Whenever you choose to retire, have a plan to stay engaged, have a daily purpose, and follow your passion!

Part of being prepared for retirement is planning for inflation. We generally adjust living expenses to increase at 3% annually. Even my most frugal clients spend more at 80 than they did at 60. It's unbelievable to some of them how much it costs to live! As a matter of fact, many people find it hard to believe how much their monthly expenses will increase over the years from inflation alone. The effect of inflation on baby boomers will be even greater than it was for previous generations, with the health care costs driving the problem. When we look at health care costs 20 years from now with a 5-6% inflation factor...the numbers are staggering!

It's critical to know how much income you'll need to maintain your standard of living in retirement. Because if you cannot maintain your standard of living, what do you have to do? Cut expenses. What goes first? The fun! What if that's not enough? Then you start cutting the basics. Maybe you don't go to the doctor when you should or don't take your medication as prescribed. Might you not eat healthy foods or stop activities you enjoy? Will all of these things affect your peace of mind or health and well-being? Absolutely they will, and I believe are likely to occur if you don't have a complete plan.

When we talk about a complete plan, there will be several components. A complete plan will include income in retirement, emergency needs, health care expenses, long-term care expense and legacy planning. The results then help us to identify the products that address these needs.

Occasionally we visit with folks who ask us, "Should I own this or that product?" Our response is always: "How is this product in alignment with the plan?" The answer to that question will determine if it should be in the plan or not. We build a plan first, and then choose the products that best help you reach your goals.

If you haven't made a plan by now, ask yourself, why? Most of our clients agree that there is a tremendous amount of uncertainty in the world. Whether it's financial, political, or personal, it can be difficult to know what direction to choose based on all the uncertainty in their life. Not knowing what will happen can lead you to not make a decision at all. Don't fall into this trap! Ask questions and move forward until you have a plan that makes sense to you.

Maybe you haven't started because it seems overwhelming and you don't know where to start. The plan is created through a process. You eat an elephant one bite at a time, and that is how our process is built. I help you each step of the way until the plan is complete. We create To-do's for you to complete at home and then we meet to evaluate. Some folks require more To-do's than others but at the end of the day, there will be a plan that fits your needs/wants/wishes, and you can know if there are holes in your plan, and you get to decide if you want to fix them.

It could be that you're afraid to see the results of the plan because of what it will tell you. Most people have a sense of what their financial future will be. Wouldn't it be better to know now than when you're retired, and the only choice then is to lower your standard of living? Many worry that they will have to work until they are 80 when that is not actually the case. Your plan will estimate your income and expense, increased for inflation, for the rest of your life so you can see what is necessary at 75, 80, 85 years old to maintain your standard of living. Then we work together to make adjustments so that you can build a successful plan.

Depending on your situation, this might mean you'll need to take money out of your nest egg, just like the McMillans. When retirement happens, some folks just cannot bring themselves to take money out of their nest egg. They have saved their whole life to build this nest egg, and the thought of removing any of it is horrifying! Some will sacrifice and go without instead of taking from the nest egg. A plan can show you how you are able to utilize your resources in a responsible manner and enjoy the early years of retirement and still be prepared for the future.

It sounds obvious, but why would the people you serve want to achieve this outcome?*

You've spent your whole life defining your idea of the perfect retirement, and you've worked each day to save for it. Now it's time to ensure you can live your retirement the way you've always dreamed.

We are dedicated to providing the best information and guidance for your retirement and financial future. We'll explain the pros and cons of everything because we believe in an unbiased, transparent approach to help you make smart decisions.

We focus entirely on your wants and needs, giving you complete attention and treat you with respect. We feel like a family here, and hope that you'll feel the same when we meet!

It's not about your money, it's about your life.

What led you to this field?

During my years as a tax accountant, I noticed that my clients who were able to contribute to IRA's were not doing so. In many cases, they were not taking other measures to plan for retirement either. That prompted me to look for ways to help them and is what brought me to becoming a retirement planner. It is tremendously satisfying to help families develop a plan and then walk alongside them as they create memories and a legacy for their children and grandchildren. As I've said, we believe, "It's not about your money, it's about your life." And we have created a process to plan this way.

What final thoughts would you like to share with the reader who wants to make their money last through retirement?

We've covered a lot of territory in just a few pages. Remember, if you want to know your money will last in retirement but are too busy, too scared or too frugal not to get help... Get help! Create a comprehensive plan that helps you know how much retirement income will be needed for you to live a successful retirement.

Understand where the holes in your plan are so you can make educated decisions about what actions to take. Leave a blueprint for your children, so they do not have to wonder if they did the right thing when they had to make the decisions. Finally, leave a legacy that will have meaning for your grandchildren and great-grandchildren.

Your plan may confirm what you already know, but chances are it will bring new insights you haven't considered that will make or break your retirement. Also, don't wait. If you've made an effort to read this book, harness that motivation before it wanes and follow through with getting your plan in place so you and your spouse can have the peace of mind to live with purpose and passion.

There is nothing more important than the choice you make right now. No one can do this for you. You have to choose to move forward, choose to call and make an appointment, choose to put your financial future ahead of all the distractions of the day. What will you choose now?

If the reader wants to know more, how can they connect with you?

I also offer a one-hour consultation to see if we are a fit and if we can help you. Additionally, we offer group meeting periodically throughout the year. If you would like to learn more about either of those options, please call the office at 970-256-1748, or see a list of upcoming meetings is on our website www.gjretire.com/workshops. We would love to meet you, come visit us!

BARBARA LANE

Retirement Income Certified Professional,
Investment Advisor Representative,
Pathfinder Wealth Management, Inc.

Email: **balane@pathfinderadvisory.com**
Website: **www.pathfinderwealth.com**
Call: **(815) 399-9806**

Barb began her financial services career in 1998, after 20 years on the accounting side of business. She felt her eye for detail, excellent listening skills and a strong commitment to her clients were an ideal foundation as a financial advisor.

In 2004, she started a retirement planning practice called Senior Capital Management, specializing in helping families with post-retirement issues such as investment management, taxation, and asset protection.

Realizing a need to offer more comprehensive retirement planning for her existing clients, she decided to merge her practice with Pathfinder in February 2011. She is passionate about helping her clients navigate and understand that retirement is a process and not a one-time event.

Barb has a strong commitment to her clients, acknowledging that her business is about valued partnership and trust. No matter what, if you are with her in the office or out as friends, you will find her to be a genuine and caring people person.

Barb enjoys volunteering for special events to "help make the community a fun, safe and healthy place to live."

A native of Rockford, she has one beautiful daughter and looking forward to having grandchildren in the future. She loves vacationing, reading, music, exercising and gardening. Most importantly to Barb are her friends and family.

PHILIP W. GUSKE

Founder, Investment Advisor Representative,

Pathfinder Wealth Management, Inc.

Email: **pwguske@pathfinderadvisory.com**

Website: **www.pathfinderwealth.com**

Call: **(815) 399-9806**

Phil began his career in 1980, after serving on active duty as an officer and US Army Pathfinder.

Initially, he was reluctant to enter the financial business because he refused to be associated with an industry known for its high-pressure sales tactics and dubious products. He changed his mind after reading Norman F. Dacey's book, "What's Wrong With Your Life Insurance?" He recognized the critical need for consumer education in the areas of life insurance and investments.

After working for several large firms, his experience led him to the conclusion that the home office encourages representatives to promote products and strategies most profitable for them, but least productive for the consumer. An investor, it seemed, had little chance of achieving peace of mind and financial security.

In 1996, he created Pathfinder as an alternative to these industry's conflict of interest and as a fee-based independent, holistic fiduciary, he had the opportunity to place the needs of the client first - not some big Wall Street firm.

Phil, his wife, Karen, two children and two grandchildren live on their farm in the Midwest. Phil is an elder in his church and an active Crossfitter.

Describe the clients you work with and the types of situations they find themselves in when they come to you for your help?

When we entered the business years ago, we were both amazed by the lack of pure financial information available to the public. In those days of TV and radio, there were plenty of advertisements for companies and products, but almost nothing that taught "why" it was important to save for the future or "how" it should be done. With the coming of the internet and social media, the public became more aware they needed to do something on their own. Social security would not be adequate, and their pensions might go by way of the dinosaur.

Today, there are millions of sources of financial information available. All this advice overload leads people to conclude that their solutions rest in the "right kind of investment" rather than understanding the threats. They come to us and ask, "Should we avoid the stock market and buy gold?" "What about annuities and life insurance?" Once they understand the greatest dangers to their future which are inflation, taxes, and excessive market risk, they can explore solutions.

The ideal client is one who demonstrates two very important things - first, it is essential that they admit "I know that I don't know how to build or protect my wealth." And secondly, they are eager and willing to be taught and implement strategies by a trusted advisor.

What are some of the challenges that prevent your clients from understanding their investments?

The average investor has never been taught how investments work, where returns come from, what the term "risk" really means and how important it is to choose an advisor acting in their best interest. Over their lifetime, they experience sales pitches from brokers, bankers, and insurance agents.

To give you an example, recently, a couple came to see us from one of our educational workshops. They had rolled over $1m from a 401-k into a product that offered guarantees and wondered if they had made the right decision. They discovered the product offered low returns and had high surrender charges. When asked if they were pleased with their purchase, they responded "no" and went on to explain that the salesman played upon their misunderstanding and fear of the stock market and did not explain the downside. A combination of fear, lack of education and sales pressure resulted in a terrible, costly outcome. They assumed they were making a "safe investment that would grow to meet financial needs."

Clients are often led to believe that investments are too complicated to understand and therefore lean heavily upon the so-called experts. Because of this mentality, many remain ill-equipped to make wise choices and fall into many "financial traps" waiting for them. And because life expectancy has increased, these wrong choices today can impact them for the next 20-30 years.

Another challenge clients face is thinking they are conservatively invested, when in fact they hold risky investments. A couple came to us thinking they were very conservative and had little exposure to the market. In fact, they held twice as much risk than was necessary for their required return. Their response was "we had no idea what was actually in our portfolio!" Such misinformation is not understood until it's too late and losses are realized.

A third big challenge facing clients is their lack of knowledge regarding taxes and how devastating it may be on their retirement. It is not an understatement that their investment returns can be double and triple taxed. It may be a great achievement to accumulate $1m in an IRA until the client realizes the tax time bomb they have created for themselves and their heirs. We often say, "the bold print giveth and the fine print taketh away," meaning, eventually the tax savings experienced early must eventually be given back.

As an example, a 65-year old couple came to us with a question about taking Social Security vs. IRA distributions. We were able to show them that it should not be a choice, but a careful blending of the two together, thus saving thousands of dollars in their lifetime.

Tax savings strategies take into consideration many aspects including income need, use of the money, charitable intent, expected risk and return and how much to leave to heirs. It is only through effective tax planning that savings opportunities can be uncovered.

How have you both helped your clients to understand their investments and make informed decisions?

We experience an enormous feeling of satisfaction to know we had a hand in getting our clients "safely on the ark" to quote financial author Nick Murray. However, as prepared as we strive to be, we were surprised one day by the news that one of our most successful clients was in trouble. A report showed that they would soon deplete their funds. The 25 years that we had projected would end in 5. At that moment, we experienced an epiphany. We realized that post-retirement clients desperately continue to need our help in controlling cash flows, investments, and planning for years ahead. We understood that absent our guidance, they could lose their financial independence. The outcome of a difficult conversation with this couple about "going to the well" too often for cars for grandchildren, extended cruises for the whole family and funded business ventures for friends brought them back to reality, and consequently to our original plan for them.

In another case, we had a client with a large 401-k balance who retired at age 63. He and his wife both had pensions, and this account wasn't needed to provide income in retirement.

We explained to them that at age 70-½, he was required by the IRS to begin taxable distributions from the account every year, and required to continue distributions when his wife and children inherited the account. After examining opportunities to help with the tax burden they were facing, we determined we could save them a considerable amount of money in taxes by converting to a Roth IRA over a 13-year period, saving them and their family over $164,000 in taxes, and tripling the amount of tax-free wealth to their children and grandchildren

What misconceptions do clients have about their investments?

One of the greatest misconceptions is clients think that their investment returns are produced by their advisor. This would only be true if the advisor is clairvoyant and can predict the "best times to buy and sell, best stocks and mutual funds to own, and the best money managers to hire." Of course, this is not possible, or at least there is no way to quantify and reproduce the results. We explain to our clients that there are two schools of thought when it comes to investing - the "Wall Street approach" and the "academic approach."

Remembering that the primary objective of Wall Street firms is to maximize their profits, making money for clients is merely incidental to their goal. On the other hand, if one becomes knowledgeable, and embraces the academic science of investing, then they have reasonable expectations of outcomes. They recognize the countries, asset classes and the real places that returns come from. The work of Nobel laureates, Dr. Eugene Fama and his "3-factor model" as well as Dr. Harry Markowitz' "Modern Portfolio Theory" are the places to begin.

Another misconception is that people don't believe they will live for 30 plus years in retirement, so they put off asking the right questions at the right time. They may think what they are currently doing possibly won't get them the results they are looking for, but they have a "bury their head in the sand," "what we don't know won't hurt" mentality. When you are preparing to retire, seek a professional, interview them, ask for referrals, do your homework. It is always a good idea to get a second opinion. If they have enough faith in their current advisor, the 2nd opinion will just reinforce their current plan.

What unknown pitfalls might your clients not be, however, should be aware of?

We also have discovered numerous pitfalls or "traps" clients need to be aware of and avoid. One is they have discussions with their family, neighbors, and co-workers about investing, instead of their advisor. Then they want to compare, having no idea what the other person is invested in, the amount of risk in their portfolio, when they will need withdrawals, their individual ages, the need for income, etc. They then make emotional decisions not realizing that investing is a lifelong process, and making quick changes could alter a perfectly sound financial plan. One of the rules of prudent investing is never making decisions when you are emotionally stressed.

One of the greatest traps clients fall into is spending their time listening to financial media. This is detrimental to their financial health! The media's actual agenda is to sell advertising and enhance their profits - not the financial success of their audience. Turn on any financial cable station and the big question discussed is "what stocks do you buy today?" An unwary public is easily lulled into a false sense of security by periodicals and newsletters that put out the latest "research", promoting gold, silver or stocks and bonds. It is often their job to frighten the investor with "apocalypse de jour" in order to peddle their product. The "10 best-performing funds last year" will not necessarily be the 10 best-performing this year.

Dalbar, a firm that studies investor behavior publishes data on how poorly the public invests vs. a simple index like the S&P 500. They say much of the underperformance is due to the fact that investors hold their funds an average of fewer than 3 years. The schizophrenic advice dished out daily in the financial press is indeed a wealth killer. Just go to www.google.com and type in "investments" to see 231 million responses.

Clients have this mistaken idea that the 500 companies represented by the S&P 500 are where the greatest returns come from. This notion stems from the financial news media which quotes its' gains or losses throughout the business day. As a result, the public believes it to be the barometer for the entire stock market. Though the S&P 500 holds some of the world's largest and best-known companies, it only represents one of many established "asset classes" or groups.

As an example, the S&P 500 holds only US large company growth stocks. It does not hold 12,000 other small or mid-size value or international companies. Business is now based upon a global economy, and 51% of the world's wealth is held outside of the US. Therefore, it is important to recognize that stocks held outside the US can produce significant returns for the investor.

What are some of your client's most common fears about even attempting to achieve their desired outcomes?

One fear is commitment. Clients will schedule an appointment and show up thinking everything they're doing is alright. As we discuss their fears and concerns, we find there are many areas they have not given attention to. However, some will leave, and the emotional side says they're ok for a while. They don't have to make any changes to anything "right now." They'll do it "later." Or they "want to think about it." This fear of commitment leads to procrastination. It's likely when they leave, the fears subside also.

Additionally, they think they can go back to their current advisor for the answers. Consequently, nothing changes.

Another common client fear is that they are going to be sold something that they don't need, can't afford and won't use. They've been taken advantage of before and are skeptical about making decisions with someone they don't know. We believe the best way to help a client overcome these fears is to take them through an educational process before they become a client.

The first step is to attend a short course taught by us at the local community college. These classes are inexpensive and run 2 hours per session for 2 weeks. During the class, no service or product is offered - only pure education on the topics of investments, insurance, budgeting, risk, pension plans, tax planning and estate planning. Students are then offered the opportunity to come in for a complimentary session to address any concerns they may have. If they determine they need additional assistance, we extend private educational sessions to them for a fixed fee.

During these sessions, custom reports will be prepared and presented. Although alternative strategies may be discussed, they will not be encouraged to change anything at that time. It is only at the conclusion of these sessions that the client may encourage us to implement the plan. We call this the "Pathfinder Process" and it is designed to give the client complete awareness of each topic and total control during each stage. Never does the client advance to the next stage, until they are comfortable and eager to do so. When clients leave with a plan in place, they sense relief and peace of mind and feel they were listened to and not judged.

It sounds obvious, but why would your clients want to have enough money for their retirement years?

The short answer is increased life expectancy and not enough money could mean living in poverty.

We've found people who have enough money they will never outlive ask the same questions as those who don't, and that is "will we run out of money?" That's the big question. We place a great deal of emphasis on continuing education that eliminates many of their fears. Once they become clients, we have regular classes where we address current market concerns and other facets of retirement and tax planning, not just investments.

As people enter the retirement phase of their lives, their focus and attention on nearly everything changes. No longer will they be going to a job or career where they commit their lives to 40 hours per week. No longer are they being called upon to employ the skills and talents they have developed throughout their lifetime.

Instead of a company giving them a paycheck for their services, they must now pay themselves from their own "nest egg." They are going from a world of a steady accumulation of assets to potential depletion. Gone is the company's medical plan and now enters Medicare, supplemental insurance, nursing home spend down and other unexpected costs. Though they were professionals such as doctors, lawyers, business owners or skilled tradesmen, they realize their professional success cannot be transferred into this new area by proxy.

Retirement is now a strange and complex world with challenges they are only moderately prepared for. Our job as their trusted advisor is to give them the education, tools, and confidence they need. The Bible says "without counsel, plans fail."

What led you both to this field?

Barb's story: Simply put, I have the heart to see people succeed and work through solving their fears. Clients come to us and have a conversation about the most important topic of their lives. They are fearful, sometimes ashamed, not knowledgeable and they need help. As they share their stories about their families and their goals and dreams, I genuinely care about these people and want to achieve the best outcomes for them and their heirs.

What are those things that motivate me and give me the greatest sense of fulfillment?

I had a client thank me for giving her the confidence she needed to retire. She said had I not shown her that it was possible for her to do so, she would have continued working at her part-time position because she had a fear of the income loss. I had to show her that she was going to be ok.

Another client just recently shared how she and her husband (whom just passed away) were so glad they came to work with us as they felt they could trust us and were very happy they moved to our firm when they did. She thanked me for taking care of them, and they both appreciate our educational approach and regular classes that we have with our clients.

Phil's story: My interest in financial education started as a young army officer while stationed at Fort Bragg. I bought life insurance from a retired Colonel that would pay my wife and two babies 20k if my parachute failed to open. This plan also promised me $35k in cash value at the time of my retirement, and I accepted the agent's counsel when he stated, "What more than that would you possibly need in retirement?"

Later, a friend of mine introduced me to someone who recommended term life insurance and mutual funds as an alternative to my $20k whole life insurance plan. For the same premium, I was able to purchase $250k of coverage and have enough money left over to invest in a mutual fund. The process was transformational for me. I saw clearly how ill-informed the public was as they were sold products that were not suitable.

After leaving the military, I continued to invest and explore the business of offering financial education to others. However, the companies I worked for did not want me to educate clients but wanted me to "sell" to them instead. Thirty years ago, I felt that the educational approach would be the key to not only my client's success as investors but my own as well. Today I can testify to the success of this approach as it has allowed me to achieve my financial goals.

I think the greatest advantage I offer my clients are not brilliant ideas, or having them master complex financial concepts. The greatest advantage is teaching them how to spot the frauds and traps that will destroy their hard-earned nest egg.

What are your final thoughts for those seeking a better understanding of their investments, so they can make informed decisions, and have peace of mind in retirement and beyond?

Barb: My final thoughts for someone to have peace of mind in retirement is work with an advisor you are comfortable with, check their website, find out what they stand for, how and who do they help? The advisor's plan is only as thorough as the information you provide. Therefore, full disclosure is important, thus work with someone you trust.

How do they get paid? The biggest misconception in the industry today is how advisors are paid. Make sure you ask a lot of questions.

Retirement is a process, not a one-time event, and therefore needs to be regularly reviewed. We are not a firm that is a one-time sit-down and we solve all your issues. It takes time and effort for us to get to know our clients and plan for them accordingly.

Phil: I would suggest that the client ask any potential advisor to explain the offerings and if they cause a conflict of interest. In other words, if they can't understand it, don't do it! Also, do not be afraid to ask for references. I recently gave a prospect five, and he called and talked extensively with each one. He heard a consistent response of "education, education, education." It's important that a prospective advisor provide this level of endorsement.

If the reader wants to know more, how can they connect with you?

To start the process to determine whether we at Pathfinder can help as you enter retirement or if you are already retired, to continue to live abundantly, we offer the following resources:

1. Contact our office to reserve a seat at our next educational venue

2. Ask for a complimentary report for the topic you are most interested in

3. Schedule a 1-hour complimentary consultation on the subject most pressing.

4. Our phone number is: (815) 399-9806

5. Website: www.pathfinderwealth.com

GARY DUELL, (CHFC)

Chartered Financial Consultant

Duell Wealth Preservation, Happy Valley &

Portland, OR

Email: **g@garyduell.com**

Website: **http://www.garyduell.com**

LinkedIn: **https://www.linkedin.com/in/duellwealthsaver**

Facebook: **https://www.facebook.com/gary.duell.3**

Twitter: **https://twitter.com/WealthSaver**

Call: **(877) 326-8337**

Gary was born in Garden City Kansas, moving with his family to Salem, Oregon at the age of five. He graduated from Willamette University in 1974 with a double major in psychology and.

Gary took a harrowing nine-month stint at Oregon State Hospital as a psychiatric security aide, ending up on the women's maximum security unit. "One Flew Over the Cuckoo's Nest" was filmed there during that time, which only added to the chaos. The experience prompted Gary to change careers. He graduated from Willamette U. again, in 1977, with an MBA.

In 1997 he earned his Chartered Financial Consultant (ChFC) designation from The American College at Bryn Mawr PA. At the time, approximately 300 hours of study and 10 hours of exams were required.

Now Gary provides comprehensive financial plans and the appropriate insurance, investments and strategies to implement them, continuing ethics education classes for insurance agents, and public seminars as well. He is currently on the faculty of Portland Community College's Community Education department to provide retirement education to pre & current retirees.

Who is your ideal client, who do you help?

I help frugal couples around the ages of 58-70, who have been good savers, build accurate and dependable cash flow plans, so they have confidence in their ability to retire- and stay retired! -without running out of money.

Because I teach adult education classes about Retirement Planning & Social Security Optimization, most of my clients have recently entered, or are contemplating retirement. Virtually all of the students in my classes feel that they're OK, that they will be able to financially survive. But they want more certainty, *they want proof.*

They're afraid they may be missing something, whether it's a strategy, a peril, or deadline. They're overwhelmed with conflicting information. Without exception, after a lot of discussion and analysis, what most of these folks want is a written and definite *cash flow plan*. And they want it from a very experienced, local fiduciary adviser. Ultimately, this is the foundation for the sense of well-being they long for.

So I help those for whom retirement is imminent, or a current reality, to get an accurate snapshot of their financial future so they can develop confidence in taking the right steps to secure that future.

What common obstacles prevent your clients from building accurate and dependable cash flow plans?

By far the #1 obstacle is **fear of the unknown**. Deluged with media designed to titillate rather than educate, most folks I see feel <u>less</u> knowledgeable than they did before they began their retirement research. For example, "those who listed Fox News as one of their news sources had overall lower levels of knowledge on the factual questions."[2] The net effect is to inflate fear of the unknown. It can be more comfortable to stick with the status quo, even if it is more stressful than it is to take positive action.

After a Social Security class several years ago, a couple came into my office for their free consultation. They hadn't done any of the homework (Personal Wealth Index & Longevity Calculator). They were both large & unhealthy looking and 67 years of age. So, without thinking it through first, I suggested "we" complete the longevity calculator for

---

[2] https://www.forbes.com/sites/quora/2016/07/21/a-rigorous-scientific-look-into-the-fox-news-effect/#755725ad12ab

each of them. When the results popped up I was aghast and didn't want to turn my screen toward them: their mortality ages were both 72. *Five more years!* Having no choice, I showed them the results. To my surprise, he said, "Well, that sounds about right." I told them they should file for Social Security immediately. And that they had plenty of money to last a "lifetime." This was a worst-case scenario that justified legitimate fear of the unknown. But had they followed the Social Security strategy they learned in class (waiting to apply until age 70) they would have missed out on three years of benefits.

After fear of the unknown is the converse, fear of **too much information**, analysis paralysis, solution pollution, factquakes[3], not knowing where to begin. Related to the first obstacle, **too much information**- *even if it is both accurate and relevant* - creates the deer-in-the-headlights look I see when attendees walk into my classes. For most, the tension between the relentless assault of old age and analysis paralysis has brought them to a class where they can be face-to-face with real people who are informed and caring. They're longing for

---

[3] i.e. information that is true but meaningless and over reported, like the Dow Jones Industrial average, unemployment figures, or the latest tweets from you know who.

reasons to take action and for people to help them take action. Appropriate action, that is.

Finally, a remaining and significant roadblock is **distrust.** It's no surprise a lot of the people I meet with have trust levels in the tank due to the first two obstacles. They don't trust their own judgment, they don't trust their feelings of confidence (if and when they have any!), and they certainly don't trust the investment community. Which is unfortunate because most of us in this business work very hard to keep up to date and to provide the best results we can for our clients.

All three of these obstacles translate into their inability to have a clear vision of their financial present and future. I visually show them where their current path leads as well as the best alternative paths so they can have confidence in their financial future.

How have you helped clients to overcome the obstacles that prevent them from building accurate and dependable cash flow plans?

The #1 challenge facing every person anticipating retirement is universal:

Developing a clear and accurate snapshot of their current financial reality. This is actually the most difficult part of the planning process. For example, if you ask Google Maps for directions to the nearest Post Office, what does the app require you to do? It requires you to enable your cell phone's location. Or at least key in your current address. <u>You cannot navigate to a destination on a map without knowing where you are</u>. So, the unequivocal, universal first step is that snapshot of your current reality. If only there were an app that would automatically show you where you are and where your financial path leads. There isn't. It takes work.

This process winnows out the chaff and forces my clients and me to focus on the facts:

1. What is your survival budget? How much do you need to be confident you'll always have a place to live, food to eat, heat and light & good medical care?

2. How much are you used to spending, living the way you want to live?

3. What is your lifespan? Have you ever taken a longevity calculator?

4. What are your beliefs about money? Do they help or hinder budgeting & saving?

5. What amount and type of assets do you own and/or inherit? Do you know the realistic income potential of those assets?

Unfortunately, the financial entertainers and money media sensationalize the irrelevant: net worth, being debt-free, average rates of return, how you compare to others and trivial strategies for getting macaroni for 89 cents a box instead of $1.29.

Retirees want to know if they have enough assets and guaranteed sources of income to keep pace with inflation, taxes, and medical care. Very few have obtained a professional, evidence-based estimate of the income potential of those assets. Even fewer have a believable long-term cash flow plan.

So, by first determining precisely where they are financially and where the path they are on leads, we can change course as necessary. And this isn't a one-time task. Annual re-navigation is essential; new obstacles crop up, and new solutions are constantly being innovated.

What common misconceptions prevent your client from having the confidence in their ability to retire, without running out of money?

Based on my best-attended class, Social Security Optimization, the most common misconception is "Social Security isn't going to be there for me." One of the best websites to learn about social security is

https://www.socialsecurityworks.org

Even before it was signed into law, Social Security was under attack by entrenched interests. And the attacks have continued over the last 80+ years. The fact is, the trust funds are at about $2.4 trillion which is enough to pay out benefits for four years *even if no additional taxes were collected*. Keep that in mind, that the trust funds are a *surplus* equivalent to 4 times annual benefits.

Another misconception about Social Security is that it's just a stack of IOU's. But the fact is that the trustees have prudently issued special T-bonds, at interest, which are 100% callable. That is, they can be redeemed in full at any time. $2.4 trillion will not fit under a mattress, let me assure you. The trustees are tasked with wisely and safely investing it. So far, they've done a stellar job.

After unfounded fears about Social Security, the next most common misconception is, "I have to endure the fear of losing money every year in order to get an adequate long-term return on my investments." *There are no guarantees that taking more risk will net you more gains.* And if you have sufficient savings, maybe you can be conservative, avoid those sleepless nights, and *still* have no risk of outliving your assets.

The next misconception I encounter is, "I will live to average age." No, you will live to the age you will live to. I **strongly** recommend you take a Longevity Calculator. Here's a good one: https://livingto100.com/calculator I have met **no one** who has done this before meeting with me. No one. Your plan needs to be scaled to your life, lifestyle, longevity, income & asset levels. If you've overestimated your lifespan then perhaps you're spending a lot less than you could. If you've *under*estimated your lifespan, then you might have to work longer, save more, and adjust your budget accordingly. As the old joke goes, you may want your check to the undertaker to bounce, but you don't want your checks to IRS or your pharmacy to bounce while you're still here.

What unknown pitfalls should your clients be aware of, no matter what situation they find themselves in?

First and foremost is <u>Taxes</u>. Taxes will be the 2nd largest expense, after healthcare. My profession has unwittingly set retirees up for this pitfall by relying too much on the old-fashioned rule of thumb that they'll be in lower tax brackets in retirement. What I'm finding is, with clients who have been successful in accumulating retirement assets and smart about creating base income cash flows (such as optimizing Social Security benefits, maximizing pensions, and developing other passive income sources such as rent) they end up paying *more* taxes in retirement, not less. So, in many cases, they've deferred income into higher tax brackets!

This pitfall can be fairly accurately assessed 5-10 years before retirement in order to answer this question: Should I max out my tax-deferred savings now, during my earning years?

But having failed that, and with retirement imminent, inappropriate tax-deferral can be minimized by a carefully crafted Roth conversion schedule between one's retirement date and age 70 when both Social Security kick in and required distributions must be taken out of retirement accounts. That way most or all deferred taxes will be paid within a window of lifetime lowest tax bracket.

To illustrate, here's a true example (names have been changed) of a couple I worked with.

Bill & Mary planned to retire this year at 62. They had accumulated about $500k in their 401(k)s. Their plan was to roll their 401(k)s into IRAs and let them continue to grow until age 70.5 when required distributions (RMDs) began. In the meantime, Bill's small pension and their combined Social Security benefits would be sufficient to meet their $4000/mo. budget. Then, as inflation compounded, their IRAs would allow them to maintain their budget. Pretty good plan. I illustrated their plan in my Road to Wealth software, and it worked out well; their money lasted until age 90. But I still considered that to be risky; their longevity calculator results were age 88 & 96 respectively. So instead, here is the new plan:

- Delay Social Security until age 70, at which point it will be nearly twice as much

- Begin immediately drawing down the IRAs up to the 15% Federal Tax bracket limit. In their case that was about $35,000/yr.

- Of that drawdown, any amounts not needed to meet their budget will be converted to Roth IRAs, or about $25,000/yr. So, by the time they reach 70.5, they will have protected $200,000 of their retirement assets from both RMDs and future taxation.

This combined strategy left them with over $300,000 to pass on to their kids at age 100 if they live that long, versus running out of money at age 90.

Next, after taxes, the most common pitfall I come across in folks is <u>Trusting without Verifying</u>. Virtually everyone is smart enough to understand their options. But financial planning is daunting. It takes guts to insist on clear, concise explanations while risking the appearance of being uninformed or dumb. But hey! That's what we advisers are here for; to educate and inform.

For example, in the past, I've rattled on in class using acronyms that I just assumed everyone was familiar with. At the beginning of each class, I encourage students to *please* interrupt me, to not fear appearing dumb, that the only dumb question is the one they don't ask, and so on. But despite that, one evening, halfway through, a woman raised her hand & asked, "What's an IRA?" Good for her!

In addition to being perfectly clear on definitions, it is even more crucial to verify the fiduciary status of your adviser and the advisory firm. Studies have shown conclusively that problem brokers tend to cluster together. They also show that some of the more prominent scams could have been avoided with a simple background check at *https://brokercheck.finra.org*

John Elway, former Denver Bronco's quarterback, is a case in point. taken for $15 million by his "investment adviser" Sean Mueller. A quick background check would have revealed Mr. Mueller's history of ripping off clients in the 90's. Elway's loss could have been avoided. Mueller's 40-year prison sentence will not bring back Elway's $15 million either. What was it Ben Franklin said, "An ounce of prevention . . ."?

After taxes and misplaced trust, I've seen that the 3rd major pitfall is <u>Fees & Expenses</u>. Costs are inevitable. But make your adviser show you the benefits are at least equivalent. In other words, if your adviser's recommended portfolio costs more than equivalent alternatives but performs worse over the long term, why would you tolerate that? All too often, when I compare a client's existing funds with the funds I use, we find that their current funds cost 2-10 times more, perform worse over the long term, and are more volatile.

Insist on a comparison *net of all fees and costs.* The key word there is "net", that is after all costs, charges, and fees are deducted.

For example, a 401(k) statement I recently reviewed showed this for the majority allocation:

Ten-Year Cumulative Returns- 66.5%

Ten Year Returns After Fees & Expenses- 33.2%

More than half of the gains in this fund had been consumed by fees and expenses! Unbelievable.

So be sure when comparing historical performance that you're getting the full story.

What common fears hold your clients back from attempting to build accurate and dependable cash flow plans, so they can have confidence in their ability to retire without running out of money?

Definitely the almost universal fear is getting taken advantage of, the emotion of misplaced trust. It is both laudable and unfortunate that consumers have grown wary of their feelings of trust. The emotion of trust is so easily elicited and manipulated that all of us have been burned in a situation we implicitly trusted. Despite the incredibly skilled cons who exploit them, investors who have been ripped off are still, out of embarrassment, reluctant to notify authorities, making it more difficult for others to protect themselves from scams. Trust but verify. Insist on the twin elements of trust: evidence and understanding. Use the Internet to research individuals and firms with whom you're considering working. Once again, https://brokercheck.finra.org is a great place to start, as well as your own State's financial regulatory agencies.[4]

After distrust of advisers, the next most common fear is expending work, fees, and expenses with no commensurate benefits. This is a corollary of the first fear, being taken advantage of. I won't sugar-coat the planning process. It takes a lot of work, and a lot of hard soul-searching as well, to figure out what you really want in life, what you care about, and what does and does not give you happiness. I understand the thought, "What if, after all those meetings, all that homework and Gary's fee, I don't feel any better off?" The only way to find out is to jump in. The risks of avoiding planning are higher! Plus, if I'm not absolutely confident I can improve your situation, I'll be the first to discourage going forward with the planning process.

---

[4] In Oregon http://dfr.oregon.gov/gethelp/Pages/index.aspx

Finally, is fear of long-term commitment. You don't want to get locked into anything or feel obligated. I understand that. That's why a great deal of flexibility is built into my plans. The longest commitment you'll ever make in the plan we develop together is for your long-term money, and that is ten years or less. And even in that case you usually still have multiple, cost-free ways to access your long-term money.

Why would your clients want to feel confident about having dependable cash flow during their retirement years?

Everyone seeks a sense of well-being. Most, however, want it to be based on reality, not delusion or baseless optimism. But there is that one out of four individuals or couples who prefer a comforting fairy tale to the reality of their situation and how it stacks up in the real world.

When I meet with clients for the first time I ask them to rank their financial situation on a scale of 1 to 10, where 1 is a total disaster and 10 is perfect. Just on a gut level. Then, whatever their score is, I ask them what it would take to increase their score to a 10. Usually, this takes quite a bit of prodding and discussion because rarely has anyone had the time to mull this over seriously. Almost always, a "10" comes down to a high confidence level that they'll have more than sufficient cash flow for the rest of their lives.

The reasons are obvious: peace of mind, security for spouse and family, lack of fear of the future and going broke. Most people fear running out of money more than they fear death! It is gratifying to help reduce or eliminate that fear.

What led you to this field?

The head nurse slathered conductive gel on his temples and then strapped the two paddles in place. To avoid chipped teeth and tongue bites a thick mouth guard was inserted, against his screams and struggles. Four large muscular aides held him down while two others secured thick leather straps on his arms, legs, and torso. She hollered, "Free," everyone backed away, and she flipped the switch. His body arched off the gurney, veins popping, while he gasped between clenched teeth.

This was Toby's (not his real name) bi-weekly electroshock "therapy". Not coincidentally, the head nurse was a Caucasian woman from the South and Toby was black, a convicted rapist, and in the men's maximum security psychiatric unit of Oregon State Hospital. Toby eventually died on that gurney.

It was 1971. To this day I'm incredulous I was required to witness this.

This was just one of countless experiences during my employment there that drove me to abandon my original career choice, psychiatry. The movie "One Flew Over the Cuckoo's Nest," based on the book by Oregon author Ken Kesey and starring Jack Nicholson, was filmed on my ward while I was there. In a dark but strangely appropriate twist, some of the staff were cast as patients, and some of the patients were cast as staff. There was indeed a very thin line between them. Both the book and the movie were mild versions of the reality I experienced as a psychiatric security aide.

Although it still haunts me more than 40 years later, that experience helped me appreciate my health, my sanity, and my freedom relative to those poor souls. It made me appreciate how petty and unfounded most of our day to day concerns are. And that gratitude has also stuck with me.

After saving up enough for the first year's tuition, I went back to Willamette University to get a master's degree in public and business administration. After graduating, I entered Farmers Insurance's management training program, on my way to becoming an insurance executive. After 3 years, my third boss told me I could either quit or get fired (she & I didn't see eye to eye). So, I became a Farmers Agent and did that very successfully for 16 years. I enjoyed helping dilute the prevailing distrust of insurance agents, and during those years I was at the top of the list for client retention. Seeking more challenge as well as more tools to help my clients I became an independent agent in 1996 and obtained my securities licenses so I could deal with all my clients' financial needs.

Having witnessed such abject suffering in that early career, my personal mission has evolved to include reducing suffering, fear, and doubt in my clients' minds and inducing rational, evidence-based faith in their retirement futures. It's my favorite thing, to prove to fearful people that they have an optimistic future!

What are some of the reasons why people who could easily benefit from working with you, might choose not to?

Cost- The average aspiring retiree is stuck in a quandary: By working with an adviser, they're making a leap of faith that the cost/benefit will be worth it. Yet there really is no way to tell in advance. That's tough. The only advice I can offer is **trust but verify; insist on evidence and understanding.** Do nothing unless you understand it. And again, unless I'm positive that I can make a significant difference, I won't proceed.

Time commitment- As much as many folks desire to just plunk down a sheaf of their statements on an adviser's desk and state, "Just do what you think is best," no adviser worth his salt will do that. Yes, some choices can be very complex. But you can hold an understanding of them at least long enough to decide which are the right courses of action.

What others would think- Most folks I meet with for the first time are initially reluctant to give me a lot of detail. That's because the media has bombarded them with so many real- and fake -examples of multi-millionaires who have done everything right. Their expectations are way too high, and their opinion of how well they've done is way too low. They're needlessly embarrassed. Seeking help is what all successful people do!

What final thoughts do you have for people who want to feel confident in their ability to retire, without running out of money?

My final thoughts for someone wanting to have confidence in their ability to retire is:

To be courageous and work with a truly holistic fiduciary to take an accurate snapshot of your current financial situation. That is the scariest step, discovering and facing your financial reality. Get expert help on finding where you are on the retirement map, where you want to go, and how to navigate to that point. Based on the thousands of folks I've worked with, you are probably in better shape than you think! Be skeptical of the financial entertainers and money "porn" magazines who tell you your "number" for retirement accumulation is $2.0 million. I deal with middle America, and only one out of ten have that much saved. With an average budget, most couples will be fine if they have $5-600,000.

If the reader wants to know more, what's the best way to connect with you?

The best place for you to start is at the beginning, with you, your beliefs, attitudes, and expectations.

Prior to meeting with me I "make" all prospective clients take the <u>Personal Wealth Index Questionnaire</u> at <u>www.personalwealthindex.com</u> Review the *What it Is, Why Take It,* and *What You'll Get* tabs first if you like. (My Advisor Code is DUE503.) I'll summarize those three tabs for you:

1. What it is- it's a comprehensive assessment of how you rank with national averages in the four cornerstones of *true* wealth: Family & Friends, Health & Wellbeing, Meaning & Purpose and, of course, Money & Finance. It does not ask for any financial numbers from you.

2. Why take it- because it helps me help you make better, wiser financial decisions.

3. What you'll get- a full color 18- page pdf report with my comments.

If you have an immediately pressing decision to make, such as Social Security timing or a looming deadline to choose the best pension options, feel free to contact me through my website contact form here:

<u>http://www.garyduell.com/contact-us</u>

Feel free to use the same contact form to request a free, 45 minute, absolutely no-obligation phone, web, or face-to-face consultation. Or call 877-326-8337. I prefer meeting in person. We have several convenient locations around the Portland Metro area.

THOMAS 'SKIP' KELLEY

President & Strategic Financial Advisor

Safe Money Retirement Strategies

Email: **info@safemoneyretirementstrategies.com**

Website: **http://www.safemoneyretirementstrategies.com**

LinkedIn: **www.linkedin.com/in/thomas-skip-kelley**

Facebook: **Safe Money Retirement Strategies**

Call: **(603) 935-9259**

A native of Lexington Massachusetts, Skip spent most of his youth growing up in Moultonboro, NH on Lake Winnepesaukee. After 28 years raising his three children, Duke, Ryder and Cody Rose in Bedford, the Kelleys now reside on the banks of the Merrimack River in Manchester. His wife of 33 years, Kathleen Rose, teaches Physical Education at Bedford High School.

Skip has been successful in a number of fields as a salesman for a Fortune 50 company, business owner, real estate entrepreneur, and investor. He believes the strategy behind investing for a comfortable retirement must be driven by safety, growth, and control. He dedicates his time to understanding each individual's financial needs and objectives, and his ultimate goal is to provide guidance and direction that result in financial peace of mind.

As a big-time sports fan, he loves following the Red Sox, Patriots and particularly enjoys rooting for UNH Wildcat Hockey and Football. Family is important to Skip, and he relishes every moment by creating lifetime memories – whether it's in his boat on the water, skiing down mountains, golfing or flying his little putt-putt two-seater Piper Colt.

Tell us about the kind of clients you work with.

The typical clients that we at Safe Money Retirement Strategies work with are primarily pre-retirees and retirees whose overriding concern is, "How do we make sure we do not outlive our money?"

They are worried, sometimes to a debilitating extent. They have not much more than a foggy concept in their minds on whether or not they will have enough money to maintain their lifestyle in retirement. It nags at them emotionally and even may affect them physically with increased stress and a knot in the stomach that does not always go away. This unease at a time which is supposed to be the 'carefree' retirement years can easily be exacerbated by a non-cooperating volatile stock market.

Our mission is to walk our clients through a comprehensive 'Income Planning Process.' A process designed to minimize the gray area of the clients' financial futures and to clarify and add black and white solutions and strategies to reduce and many times eliminate the emotional angst they may carry. In the end, this planning process is specifically designed to provide our clients a rare and precious commodity, increased peace of mind!

***In order to achieve this outcome, there will be some obstacles we
must clear.***

First, we must understand if we can retire? Most potential
clients do not know if they have enough wealth accumulated
to successfully maintain their lifestyles in retirement. Even
after successfully accumulating these assets over their
working lives they have no idea how they can 'distribute'
those monies at a rate that can ensure it will last their
lifetimes.

So just how can we make it last? With all the financial land
mines in retirement such as inflation, taxes, Social Security
woes and the insane rising Healthcare and Long-Term Care
costs among other issues, how can our clients confidently
allocate their resources and create income streams designed
to maintain their lifestyles and guarantee they will not outlive
their money.

Another obstacle to financial security that most of us do
not recognize is the issue of having available to us too much
information... In a world ruled by Google, how can you as a
client know you are on the right track when a search for any
financial topic immediately garners you over two million
responses? Half the info will seem to support, and the other
half will annihilate any strategy. In these instances, too much

information may lead you to screw yourself into the ground. Good gravy Martha, what and who do we believe? And just what does a confused mind do? Nothing!

So just how do we assist our clients in overcoming these obstacles to financial security and peace of mind?

In order to keep our office humming with appointments we do a lot of marketing including a weekly radio show and also dinner seminars at least every other week to let folks get acquainted with us and determine if they believe it prudent to come into our office and continue the conversation. If they do come in it is because they have needs and questions they want answered.

Many of our clients originally came to us as they looked at their portfolio, saw that on average 90% of their wealth was invested in the market, and then had to take a swig of Maalox to settle their indigestion. That remedy gets old, so eventually they might acquiesce and set an appointment to see if this financial doctor can fix what ails them.

Another major bone of contention these folks who come to see us have is their inability to fully understand if they have or will have a built a nest egg large enough to actually retire, or better yet, be able to maintain their lifestyle in retirement.

I am an Income Planner, that's what we do.....we take the gray out of your financial future and make it black and white. First, we reduce the risk in the portfolio creating 'safe money' accounts. Then we create guaranteed income streams we can utilize in the future to augment your Social Security, pension and other income streams as our expenses rise due to inflation. Finally, we reallocate the 'risk' monies invested in the market. Because we have addressed the percentage of the risk in the portfolio already and are hedged for safety, the monies we leave diversified in the market will be invested aggressively for maximum upside. It is a highly comprehensive process designed to specifically answer all the individual family's needs.

There is nothing like the end of the decision-making meeting where the clients have seen the plan, understood, and appreciate the benefits and cannot wait to put it into effect. If you listen closely, you can actually hear the stress leave the room.

Many folks have misconceptions about the planning process and what to expect.

The first misconception is that this is going to be a painful process and I'm just not ready to deal with it.

This is not ordinarily a painful process, but it does require time, thought, work and decision-making. The process can take 3 to 6 meetings depending on the client's specific financial complexities and will culminate with an effective Income Plan both the client and the Advisor will use as a roadmap in each future meetings as the years unfold ahead. This effort will bring forth a clarity and peace of mind. You will wonder why you waited so long to address this situation.

Another misconception I see is that folks have the idea that they must be loyal to their current Advisor whether the results have been good or bad. This is what I inevitably hear, "We have been working with my Advisor for years, and he/she is such a nice person.

I have never had a potential client tell me that their current Advisor was anything less than 'very nice'. Ok, I get that, but is that really the issue? A couple of quick questions for you. Each meeting when you go through and update your income plan with your current 'good guy' Advisor....no wait, what.... this plan has never been put in place....yet....after years of 'managing' your monies???

OK then, so tell me, what are the guarantees your current 'good guy' Advisor has given you regarding how much wealth you will have accumulated by retirement? How much income does he guarantee you can generate to augment your retirement income streams such as your Social Security and pension incomes? Really? He doesn't guarantee anything?

One last misconception I see when folks first come to us for help is that this Skip guy has only one itinerary and that is to sell me an annuity.

Uuuuughhhh!

Just because every dinner seminar you have ever attended but also every other commercial you see these days is about the importance of having annuities in your portfolio... Selling you an annuity is not Skip's primary goal.

First of all, as a Series 65 registered Investment Advisor Representative, I am a Fiduciary. Anything I discuss or advise must be in your best interest, not mine. I do not use a sales process, I use an education process. It is an in-depth evaluation of your financial circumstances, a complete risk assessment of your current portfolio, a thorough survey of your personal goals and lifestyle requirements in retirement. It all culminates in an in-depth, specific, comprehensive income game plan for your future.

As a holistic Income Planner, I can manage both your risk assets (market securities such as stocks, bonds, mutual funds,

ETFs) and your safe money assets (insurance instruments such as fixed index annuities and/or life insurance). Holistic means we look at your entire portfolio with an eye on risk and act accordingly. Every client has a different threshold of risk they can confidently live with. It is not how I feel about your risk threshold, it is about how much risk you can comfortably accept and are willing to employ. I can only lead a horse to water.

In any case, when we decide how little or how much risk you are willing to take, then and only then will financial instruments be discussed... and yes, maybe annuities will be a part of that conversation.

So what are some of the pitfalls one should be aware of when selecting an Advisor?

Pitfall #1 is Your Broker.......where does your nice guy Broker tell you to invest all of your nest egg......the market of course! Stocks, bonds, mutual funds, REITs.....it is the 'only' place to get any type of reasonable rate of return. It matters not your age, your retirement horizon, your goals, or future income you'll need......into the market it goes, risk, and your future lifestyle be damned.

Pitfall #2 is Your Broker....if you've been to a dinner seminar put on by a broker you have no doubt been pushed to 'diversify' and fund a future income stream in the form of a Variable Annuity. Yes, a Variable Annuity will guarantee you a future income stream, but it does not protect your investment principal. The problem is that your monies are at the risk of the market as they are 100% invested in 'sub-accounts,' quite similar to mutual funds. Understand these are securities, not insurance products.

Another major problem with these instruments is that in order to enjoy any principal gain the market must be in cooperation and grant you a sizable annual increase to overcome the gargantuan fees buried in the contract. The typical fees on average total 3.5% annually for a Variable Annuity... that is a large hump to overcome in a good year, never mind a year your sub-accounts may have lost money. This makes it very hard to gain positive traction in your account.

Pitfall #3 is Your Insurance Agent......so if a Broker can only help you with Securities, which are risk instruments, what do you expect your Insurance professional will talk to you about? That's right, insurance products, or safe money instruments! Typically these instruments would be in the form of Fixed Index Annuities or Life Insurance. Both can be great products but is that where all your monies should reside?

How can either one of these Advisors, the Broker or the Insurance Agent look at your portfolio and holistically advise you in a manner to your best interest? Simple answer, they can't.

Now tell me, what are some of the most common fears about even attempting to achieve the ultimate goal of financial peace of mind?

One fear would be you won't even know where to begin to understand if you have saved enough for retirement and certainly don't want to look foolish in front of your Advisor if you come up short. Sticking your head in the sand will not answer your questions nor improve your peace of mind. Get with the program kid and begin the process of discovery and get that comprehensive income plan in the works. Know if you've got enough money saved to live the life you want in retirement and know that your portfolio is designed to the proper levels of risk which will guarantee your financial plan to carry you through to the very end.

Another fear is that you will feel less than intelligent if you defy your Broker's advice and transition any funds out of the risk of the market and... certainly will feel disloyal if you move monies out of his management.

My broker says the only place to have my wealth is in the market as it is the only place I can get reasonable rates of return, he is incorrect! Not only is he incorrect but he also cannot give me ONE (1) guarantee in regards to my account balance at any point in the future nor can he guarantee me how much income I can take safely to augment my income in retirement without running out of monies as long as I am breathing.

As for feeling guilty about potentially transitioning some of your funds to another Advisor who will create a holistic portfolio plan, a plan working with both risk and safe money investments, guilt is not necessary. This is your money we are talking about, and you have to do what is in your family's best interest, not your Brokers.

A final common fear occurs when you have heard and read so many negative comments about the 'safe money' insurance products such as Fixed Index Annuities and Life Insurance, why would I ever spend one minute trying to educate myself on those crummy products?

Maybe you shouldn't take the time to educate yourself. Listen to your Broker, he is such a good guy........ He wouldn't lead you down the wrong path. He will be right there with you the next time the market tanks to hold your hand and reassure you, "Don't worry, the market always comes back." "Don't worry, you're not alone, everyone is losing money." "Don't worry, we're in this for the long haul."

Not very satisfying when you've busted your butt to build your nest egg over decades of hard work only to watch it slowly diminish before your very eyes each time the market decides to take a swan dive. Those monies were supposed to maintain your lifestyle in retirement and support you through your final chapters.

Think about this, the Broker, who can offer you only risk for your assets, can offer you no guarantees whatsoever, none, is the Advisor you rely on for your 'forever' monies? The same person who is remunerated and whose personal best interest is best served by making sure you keep your monies fully invested in the market? Yep, that's the guy to listen to!

Now think about this, you have to be diversified, you have to have monies invested in the market. The question is how much. Contrary to the forces of Wall Street we cannot afford to leave all of our wealth in the risk of the market. We must diversify a portion of our portfolio to safe monies and the guarantees they can afford us.

Some might say, this is just too much, why don't I just keep doing what I'm doing?

So why would you ever upset the applecart, your Broker or your Insurance Agent by beginning a conversation with a holistic Financial Advisor specializing in retirement income planning? Gee, I don't know, peace of mind maybe.

You know your current Advisor has never prepared an income plan for you. He has no idea if the funds required to maintain your lifestyle will be there when you need them. You also know you have that queasy mixed feeling of hope in regards to your financial future. Put some certainty into your future! Give yourself the most powerful gift of peace of mind. Retirement is supposed to be your time to enjoy, it is not supposed to be a time of financial pain, mental anguish or emotional turmoil because you did not plan out the final chapters intelligently.

Do not do what retirees did in the last two market dips of 2001 (S+P decline 49%) and 2007-2009 (S+P decline 56%). They lived like chickens on a rotisserie, slowly roasting for months on end and if they needed to tap into funds to maintain their lifestyles while their accounts were being decimated by the deflating markets, their lives were never the same. The accounts they used to augment their income would not have the critical mass to recover regardless of how well the market may recover. Your story can very easily be very different.

Peace of mind is an attainable commodity, but it does not happen by accident.

What winding path led me towards becoming a holistic Financial Advisor?

I first got involved in the field of Income Planning by accident. After a multi-decade highly successful career in sales with a Fortune 50 company, (International Paper), followed by entrepreneurial pursuits in both business ownership and Real Estate acquisition I thought I had found my niche in Futures Trading. I made a terrific living for 11 years. That was until 2009 when market volatility found an all-time low and remained there for 3 or 4 years. Every trader understands that without volatility you cannot make a living. I figured I'd continue to trade mornings (peak volatility time) and utilize my sales expertise in the afternoons. I knew then that I needed to do something different. I became licensed in insurance and then securities and have never looked back. The last few years has been a satisfying evolution of learning, growing, and expansion. I have been very fortunate to early on have lucked into a couple of mentors who can only be classified as the best in the business.

What I have learned from the time I began in this business to now is monumental. As a Series 65 registered Investment Advisors Rep, that makes me a Fiduciary, a professional who is legally obligated to work only in your best interest. It also allows me as one of a very small percentage of Advisors who can work with your portfolio on a holistic basis, that being both your Securities (risk monies) and Insurance products (safe monies). In the end, we have put a comprehensive financial income plan together that gives you the client not only clarity but more importantly, peace of mind. It is a very fine feeling knowing to the marrow of my bones that once I had made a new client that their family is in a much better position than where they were before we met. How nice a way to make a living is that! I wished I had found this business 30 years ago.

So now what?

My final thoughts for someone wanting to put structure and clarity into their financial future and at the same time benefit from a powerful dose of peace of mind is to take the first step in the process of discovery........or......

You are a procrastinator. Do so at your own risk. You already know that never works out well for anyone.

You don't have the time. Ok, see you in our next life.

Your current Advisor is such a 'nice' guy! Yes, and he will hold your hand during the next market correction and tell you to hang in there. Hello, he has never put an income plan together for you yet, and he has NO guarantees for you either, but that is fine.

The only place to get reasonable rates of return is in the market. Yes, that's what I hear too, I wish you the best.

Safe Money instruments from insurance companies such as Fixed Index Annuities and Life Insurance are horrible places to put any of my money. I hear it every day on the radio, and anywhere I research in Google. They will lock my money up for years, and the rates of return are pitiful, and they have huge surrender fees if I want my money back......why I hear they even voted for Trump....... fuhgeddaboudit!

That's right, those horrible life insurance companies are terrible to work with, they give bonuses, reasonable rates of returns, allow penalty-free withdrawals, any monies left over and not paid out to you during your life will go probate free to your beneficiaries and offer guarantees you can find nowhere else...including guarantees never to lose one dime of your principal and even better, guaranteed income for life....no matter how long you live...I hate them too!

If you have retirement on the horizon or are already retired and:

- still have financial question marks in your portfolio

- don't know how much you can safely spend without running out of money

- are angst-ridden in that you have no idea if your retirement dreams are possible

- have stress and worry every day that the market may not be where you need it to be when you need it be

Give us a call at (603) 935-9259 and let's have a brief chat to see if it makes sense to continue the conversation........... Peace of Mind can be that easy!

GARY DAHLQUIST, RICP

President and Founder

Clarity Retirement Advisers, LLC

Email: **gary@clarity123.net**

Website: **www.clarity123.net**

Call: **(913) 674-5350**

Gary's company, Clarity Retirement Advisers, LLC is an independently licensed Registered Investment Advisory firm with the state of Kansas. He believes being independent is critical in today's financial climate, in that it allows him the freedom to offer clients the best, most innovative, cutting-edge principal-preservation solutions from top-rated financial companies, as well as conservative, low-risk, low volatility money managers for his clients. This allows his clients to protect their assets and reach their guaranteed income planning goals.

Gary was one of the first individuals in 2012 to receive the Retirement Income Certified Professional designation from the American College. The RICP is a year-long college course focused solely on the challenges that a 30+ year retirement creates for retirees. Gary is a member in excellent standing with the National Ethics Bureau, the Society of Financial Service Professionals, and the National Association of Financial Advisors.

He is a lifelong Johnson County resident living currently in Olathe KS. He has one daughter, Riley who is a pre-nursing student at the University of Kansas and his son Luke is a senior at Olathe Northwest High School.

Describe the clients you work with and the types of situations they find themselves in when they need your help?

We at Clarity Retirement Advisers, LLC help 55 -70-year-old conservative individuals and couples who are looking for a low risk, low volatility solutions designed specifically for their retirement. They have done a good job of saving for their golden years, but are looking for straight honest answers on how to effectively navigate the challenges of a 30-year retirement. Our goal is to get all of their concerns and questions on the table first. Then educate them on the potential pros and the cons of their current situation. We believe that most clients have no idea of the potential risks and pitfalls that are hidden in their current holdings. We walk our clients through a co-design process that gets their questions answered, so they are comfortable with their financial plan, not ours.

Our co-designed financial planning process goal is to create client peace of mind.

This co-design process is much more than asking 10 or 12 YES or No questions. We ask a lot of personal questions to determine your retirement goals and dreams. Then we delve deeper to determine your views on money and its purpose.

Look to see if and when you will run out of money. What will happen financially to the surviving spouse when a spouse passes away? The biggest thing we figure out is; does your current portfolio risk profile really match your tolerance for losses inside your portfolio.

Most clients didn't realize that their investment portfolio would go down 40 or 50% in the Great Recession of 2008. until it was too late. I blame their adviser of not educating their clients about the potential downside of their investments. An appetite for portfolio losses changes over time. A 30-year-old working for another 35 years can handle the market's up and down a lot easier than a 60-year-old's retiring in 5 years. Clients need to know how their current portfolio is built to react to a bull market but more importantly how big their losses will be in the next bear market.

What common obstacles hold your clients back from achieving peace of mind during retirement?

The biggest obstacle that I see when I meet someone for the first time is that changed their savings and investment strategies when getting close to retirement. They don't have a holistic financial plan that is built specifically for their retirement years. These retirement accounts must shift from accumulating wealth to generating lifetime income.

When you are working the plan is quite simple. Just max out your 401k's or Roth IRA accounts. Pay down debt and save as much money as possible. When you retire your steady paycheck disappears creating a brand-new set of problems and concerns. Retirees need answers to questions like:

- Will we outlive our money?

- When should we take social security?

- Which Medicare plan is right for us?

- Do I have any estate planning, needs?

- How will I generate income?

Plus numerous more. All of these questions can only be addressed by a new financial plan.

The second obstacle is that most people have accumulated a lot of different stuff in their Investments accounts. They don't know why they were sold each mutual fund or the actual cost of their holdings. Most people believe that they have these wonderful portfolios specifically designed exclusively for them. But the truth is they have been sold a Cookie Cutter portfolio. Their advisers can only offer or sell them a few select mutual fund that has been hand-picked by their company. If the fund isn't on this pre-approved list, they don't sell it.

In 2016, there were 9,511 mutual available in the United States; yet a typical large broker house statement that I see contain the same 10-15 mutual funds. I call this the Broker Profits First Portfolio Model. This model of using only pre-approved funds ensure that the firm makes money in transaction costs, ongoing fees; some of which are disclosed and some that are hidden inside the fund prospectus. Brokers are trained only to tell you the positives of the fund and gloss over the drawbacks. If the client was told everything about the proposed investment, they might question owning it.

The last obstacle that I see over and over again is that clients are taking on entirely too much risk in their accounts. They say that they are conservative but upon further analysis that just isn't the case. A 30-year-old working for another 35 years can handle a lot of market volatility and market ups and downs, but NOT a 60-year-old retiring in 5 years. The clients need to change their mindset from one of accumulation and growth to a mindset focused on preservation of principal and generating income. Their retirement nest egg needs to generate income and for 30-35 years. It needs to be able to handle all types of market conditions. Not many retirees can afford to have their portfolio lose 30-40% in a year.

Share some examples of how you've helped past clients to avoid or overcome impossible obstacles?

I had a husband and wife come meet me after ending an educational workshop. The wife was concerned about not having enough money to retire on and that they were taking too much risk. The husband, on the other hand, assured me everything was just fine; after all his account went up 12% last year. The wife thought that getting a second opinion portfolio review would be a good idea. I agreed to do a no cost, in-depth retirement MRI on their investment accounts because the needed a written retirement plan.

The MRI process is very similar to a medical doctor's assessment process. We analyze every aspect of their financial situation, run several tests to get an overview of their financial health. The results of financial diagnosis are quite simple and usually eye-opening. We review the pros and the cons their current plan. Then talk about options or small changes that can improve their situation.

The MRI revealed that they owned "A" & "C" shares mutual funds exclusively. They were actually paying close to 3.2% in all account fees, not the 1% AUM fee their broker kept assuring them. They were entering retirement with a "Buy and Hope" investment strategy. Their "Conservative Portfolio" of stocks and bonds was set up to lose 48% in the next 2008-like market correction. This was completely in opposition to how they thought were invested. But the biggest shocker was that without a spending and income plan they were on course to run out of money in 17 years. This was quite an eye-opener.

We met a couple more times and came up with a co-designed plan that addressed all their concerns. We implemented a budget, created spending and income plan. The co-designed plan included how to best pay for health care, their estate plans, and legacy goals. The holistic plan allowed us to make some slight adjustments to the original plan and got their retirement off on solid footing. They created a plan specifically for their needs giving them greater peace of mind for retirement.

What misconceptions do your clients typically have about their money and investments?

Misconception #1 is that large brokerage firms are the only people or places that should be managing my money and investments. You see these companies advertising all over the TV, in magazines, they sponsor sporting events, some companies even have blimps and large animal as their logo. So, they must be the best and only place for my hard-earned money. Stop! Hold on! You need to ask yourself, "Who is paying for all of this expensive advertising?" I mean is not free.

The answer is their clients are paying for it. The company's Profit First Model makes sure they get paid. Brokers work for their firm first, if they don't follow the company marching orders. The broker gets fired. A small independent firm doesn't answer to a board of directors. They aren't worried about corporate profits or share price. A small independent firm can offer any product or solutions with the client's best interest in mind.

Misconception #2 "Buy & Hold" portfolio is the best solution for a retiree. This Buy and Hold strategy is truly outdated. The S&P 500 lost 30% in 1987, another 45% loss in

2001-02, another 39% in 2008. The brokerage houses don't care if you lose money as long as the money stays fully invested with them. Their objective is to hold onto the largest amount of money for the longest period of time, so they can make the most amount of profits. Their motives or business plan really is that simple

There is another option called tactical management. The Tactical manager's goal is to capture 75% of market upside while only participating in 25% of Market downturns. These managers have the same mindset of most conservative investors. They want to make positive returns during the good times and get out of the market during the bad times. It is all about managing downside risk. Successful investing is more about protecting your money from devastating losses than achieving spectacular gains. If you don't have big losses; you don't need huge gains to make up for the losses.

Misconception #3 Another big misconception perpetrated by the investment / mutual fund world is that average rate of returns is extremely important. **It's another smoke and mirror tactic that doesn't really mean that much.** Investors should pay attention the Compound Annual Growth Rate called the CAGR for short. to the actual performance return on their statement and not the 3, 5, 7-year average return numbers Let me explain what I mean.

Suppose you invested $1000 at the start of the year in ABC mutual fund. The fund did extremely well, and it ended up the year worth $1500. The fund did great and had a 50% gain or a positive rate of return of 50%. The next year things didn't go so well, and the fund lost 50% or had a negative 50% rate of return. The 50% loss meant your shares in ABC fund now was worth only $750.

Here's where the average rate of return fuzzy math comes into play. You had a 50% gain in year 1; followed by a 50% loss in year 2. This gives you an average 2-year rate of return was 0%. CAGR is calculated a little different. Your account gained $500 in year 12 and then lost $750 in year 2. This left your actual account value $250 in the hole. The CAGR for this 2-year period was a negative 12.5%. Wall St. wants you to believe you had an average rate return of 0% when you actually received a -12.5% real rate of return. Investors need to pay attention the CAGR number to be successful

What unknown pitfalls or mistakes should your clients be aware of?

Pitfall #1 Mutual funds can NOT manage your money in market corrections. The mutual fund can't protect and don't manage your money during market downturns. The industry has to follow strict rules and guidelines within their prospectus. The SEC rule called 35d1; states that mutual funds must be fully invested (65-80%) of funds at all times. The funds companies can NOT sell your position during a bear market correction. The rule is trying to prevent a mass exodus causing the market to collapse. Therefore, you have to get to enjoy the losses hoping for a recovery in your account. The S&P 500 lost 43.7% in the 2001-03 tech bubble bear market and took 8 years to recover the losses. Let's not forget the S&P lost 56.3 % in the 2008-09. A tactical manager can avoid these losses because it isn't bound by the SEC 35d1 rule. They can sell when their timing models say SELL and move into the safety of CASH.

Pitfall #2 ETF will protect me from market losses. Wrong! ETF's may be a more tax efficient vehicle but are similar to mutual funds in the way they invest. ETF's use a basket of stocks within the sector they choose to invest in. SPY is an

EFT that holds the same position as the S&P 500 index mutual fund It makes the same upside gains and incurs the same downside losses. The ETF manager is NOT going to SELL the fund in a downturn. You have to call your broker or fund company and tell them to sell. A tactical manager will do this automatically within his investment model. His #1 rule is to protect investment principal and NOT lose money.

Pitfall #3 Beware of advisers holding multiple security licenses. If you sell investments in the United States, you have to have a security license, or you go to jail. Advisers with series 6, 7 or 63 are paid a commission on sales. The products they sell to consumers only have to be suitable. Advisers that hold a series 65 license get paid a flat fee for advice typically 1% of total account value. They do not receive a sales commission on security products. They also are held to the much tougher Fiduciary standard.

The fiduciary standard makes sure that the adviser offers products that are not only suitable but are in the best interest of the client. The fiduciary adviser is on the same team with the same goal as the client. They both share in the upside gains as the account value goes up and they both feel the losses when account values decrease. Beware of advisers with multiple licenses that give the appearance of being a fiduciary, but also get paid commissions. These multiple licenses can create a conflict of interest between their companies get paid first business model and doing what is in the best interest of the client. Working with an adviser who holds only a series 65 license ensures they will act in your best interest. You need to know exactly how your broker is getting paid. It's all about the license they hold.

What are some of your clients' biggest fears about investments and retirement?

Common Fear #1

One fear I see a lot from clients is that they feel that no one cares as much as they do about their money. This then leads them to think can do a better job managing their own investments. Owning one hot stock or getting lucky one year doesn't mean you can get superior returns over the next 20-30 years. An independent research firm called DALBAR has analyzed actual investment returns of investors for the last 23 years. The study results show that over the last 10 years the "average equity investor" earned only 3.6% in the market while S&P earned 6.96%. The actual underperformance by over 3% proves that average investor is good at buying high and selling low.

Common Fear #2

The second common fear is tied into the first one in that some clients just don't want to pay any fees. They feel that any management fee they pay is taking money out of their pocket. After all, they can buy the same stocks or mutual funds as the adviser online at a lower cost. So where is the value in using an adviser? Buying is the easiest part of any investment. Knowing when to sell is where it can get tricky.

Let me give you an example of why an investor should NOT be caught up solely on fees.

Let's say at the start of 2008 you invested $100,000 in the S&P 500 and paid no fees. The S&P 500 lost 37% of its value, or you lost $37,000. But what If instead you invested that $100,000 with a tactical manager that I used and paid a 2% fee or $2,000. Ouch, no way I am paying that much in fees. But here is where the value of paying a fee came in. This manager was out of the market for the entire year. Your account value lost no money. You started the 2009 bull market with $98,000 instead of $ 63,000. Fees are important.

Fees without value should be avoided. But, can you see the value in paying fees?

Common Fear #3

The hardest fear some clients to overcome is the fear of change or staying with the status quo. They don't want to go thru setting up new accounts, signing paperwork, and then having to break up with their current adviser. I hear them say all the time. Bob is such a great guy. We have been with him for 15 years, I don't want to hurt his feelings. Bob is a great guy. He is just stuck in a lousy system. The system he chose to be a part of places his company's financial well-being ahead yours. You need to get all the facts about your investment portfolio. Then you can decide what is in your best interest.

Why would the people you serve want to have low risk, low volatility solutions designed specifically for their retirement?

Client peace of mind is the result of a holistic financial plan built specifically for the retirement years. You need a well-thought plan that addresses all of the unknowns and what ifs for a retirement that may last 30 to 40 years. Can you imagine taking a 7 or 10-day vacation without starting with a plan? You don't just go to the airport and hop on the first plane that is leaving to who knows where. You start with a plan.

Nobody wants to be stressed out up at night worrying about the what if's that the future might hold. Clients need to take ownership and be an integral part of the co-design process. A good plan will help ensure that clients can keep their same standard of living and keep on enjoying life. The result will be clients that are able to sleep well at night regardless of what the future may hold. Remember not having a plan is planning to fail.

What led you to this field?

It was 1987 when the movie watching world got introduced to Gordon Gecko in Wall ST. I had just recently graduated from college and started my journey as a small business owner. This movie really fascinated me as I had always been a numbers and finance guy. I read countless books on the investing, stock picking and trading. Online trading platforms were starting to pop up on the internet, and I just knew that the stock market was going to make me rich. Someone got rich alright it just wasn't me or the little guy on Main St. it was guys like Gordon Gecko on Wall St.

The real story is that the investment world is set up to benefit the investment world not you or me. A close childhood friend of mine father lost everything he had because of bad investment advice. He was forced to move into his son's basement at the age 75. This wasn't the outcome they planned on. I have seen nest eggs drop over 50% in the dot.com crash of 2001-2003 causing tremendous amounts of stress. This was followed by another whopping 37% loss in portfolio value in 2008. All of this devastation was caused to families by following the bad advice of so-called experts.

What are your final thoughts for the 55 to 70-year-old conservative individuals and couples who are looking for straight honest answers on how to effectively navigate the challenges of a 30-year retirement?

There's only one way to make sure that you will have retirements of your dreams. You need to create a financial plan if you don't have one already. If you have one, you need to have it reviewed and explained to you in a non-biased way. The objective is not to meet with you and tell you all your investments are good or bad. Our objective is to educate you with a thorough investment and retirement analysis based on third-party information. Small changes can sometimes create huge benefits to a portfolio or financial plan.

Remember you don't know, what you haven't been told. When would you like to find out if you have a potential problem? Before it happens when you can correct it or after it happens and it's too late to fix. A second opinion helps educate you what is good in your existing plan and what might be problematic. You should only make changes to your plan only if it improves your situation.

If the reader wants to know more, how can they connect with you?

If someone wants to know more about my firm and me. I offer a no-cost 45-minute initial consultation. This initial visit can be done in person at my office or remotely over the internet. The goal of this meeting to get to know each other, find out your concerns, what worries you have, what you have done for retirement and see if there's a fit between you and me. If we both think a second meeting would be beneficial; we schedule a second meeting. During our next visit, I will be a very candid discussing all the good and bad of your current situation. If you don't like what you see and hear we part as friends. If not, we schedule another meeting to discuss possible solutions to improve your existing plan retirement.

I can be reached M- F 9- 5 at (913) 674-5350 or by email at gary@clarity123.net.

KURT ARSENEAU

Financial Advisor
Arseneau Advisory Group

Email: **kurt@arseneauadvisory.com**
Website: **www.arseneauadvisory.com**
Website: **www.healthcarecostalert.com**
LinkedIn: **www.linkedin.com/in/kurtarseneau**
Facebook: **www.facebook.com/kurt.arseneau.9**
Instagram: **kurtarseneau**

Kurt Arseneau is the CoFounder of Arseneau Advisory Group, a full service financial services office in Cumming, Georgia. Kurt and everyone at Arseneau Advisory Group believe in the client first mentality.

As a Fiduciary, Kurt is bound by law to put the client's needs first above all else. While committing to the Fiduciary standard, we begin with a holistic and unbiased approach to developing a full financial plan. Kurt believes that paying less to Uncle Sam is the cornerstone of creating a strong financial plan. Kurt has been a financial professional for over 15 years and continues to be passionate about helping clients not only in Georgia but all over the country.

In his 15+ years, Kurt has owned and operated over 5 privately held businesses, including a financial services marketing organization that generated millions of dollars in revenue.

Kurt currently lives in Cumming, Georgia with his wife Brynn and his 4 beautiful girls. While not spending time with his awesome family, Kurt participates in many sports activities and stays active in his Church. If you don't find him at the office, he is normally with the family at the pool, park, or watching a great kid friendly movie.

Describe the clients you work with and the types of situations they find themselves in when they come to you for your help?

I help 40 to 75-year-old high-income earners and business owners to reduce their overall tax liability to Uncle Sam. I like to help these individuals by lowering their taxes which in turn will increase their profitability and create and grow their wealth.

I believe that if you get the taxes wrong, nothing else really matters! The ideal client for me is someone who is willing to get outside of the box and take a hard look at what they are really doing for tax planning.

By doing tax planning and not just tax preparation, our individual clients not only put more money in their pockets today but also for the future and retirement. Also, for our business owner clients, by working with us they are able to put much more money into their business, money that was normally going to their favorite uncle, Uncle Sam.

What barriers prevent the high-income earners and business owners you work with from reducing their overall tax liability to Uncle Sam?

There are many obstacles that prevent my clients from reducing their overall tax liability, but without a doubt, the top obstacle is trust. Most individuals and business owners have a CPA or Accountant that they have been with for years. It can be a big step for someone to trust a new professional with their taxes. I am in a profession that has a reputation of being untrustworthy. We have had the Bernie Madoff's, the Jordan Belfort's, and even the large corporations like Enron, who have made us all very nervous about the financial services industry. It is very easy for people to hang on to the negative stories in the marketplace. In the fast-paced world, we live in today, the negatives always stick with us longer than the positives. If you take a step back and look at your own life, you remember the bad times much easier than the good times, it's just human nature.

Obstacle #2 - As mentioned earlier, we live in a fast-paced world where we don't have time to look at our overall financial situation, until it is too late. If we aren't running to the next meeting at work or the next networking dinner, we are at the soccer field, travel basketball game, the dance recital, or at a barbecue. It can be very time consuming to sit down and figure out what you are doing for "Your Financial Journey." The journey that you are on is ever changing and needs to be visited on a regular basis to make sure you are on track with your goals and dreams. If you don't own a business, you need to look at your family as a business. If you run the family finances as a business with balance sheets and profit and loss statements you will much further ahead, financially than any of your neighbors or friends. When you get outside of individual financial planning and get into businesses, time is even more scarce. If you are running your own business, you might be the salesperson, the marketing director, the bookkeeper, and even the janitor. You end up working in your business, instead of on your business. This mentality is a huge mistake and can cost you 100s of thousands of dollars over the course of your business.

Obstacle #3 is - Fear of change. Most of us have been burned by someone in the past. Whether it is a boyfriend or girlfriend, a set of knives we bought from someone that knocked on the door, or even a trusted friend. It just happens, it isn't right, but it is life. Same is true in the financial services industry, change is hard, and change is scary. I once heard that anything worth doing is scary and to love and lost is better than to never have loved at all. If you remember those words, change and fear become much more manageable. The fear of change usually becomes paralyzing, which makes it very difficult to help people. We aren't very scary at all, just good people looking to make a difference in a person's life. If we can't help you, we will tell you not to change anything, but if we can, we will walk with you every step of the way.

How have you been able to help high-income earners and business owners to successfully avoid those obstacles and increase their profitability, and create and grow wealth?

We recently had a business owner come to us as a referral. He had been with his CPA for over 10 years, who happened to be his cousin. He trusted his cousin with everything from tax preparation, bookkeeping, and even the payroll. The fear of coming in and seeing someone else and facing the family afterward was completely overwhelming for him. We sat down with this individual and discussed what his current business makeup was and why he came into see us. He said that his friend, who was in the same business in a different part of town, used us and said that we saved him a ton of money in taxes.

He knew we had a free assessment that we provided, and he wanted to see what was possible, but there was no way he would be changing from his CPA cousin (trust and fear). We told him no problem, let's run the assessment and see what's possible. The assessment came back, and it showed a potential tax savings of $20,000. His eyes became really big, that's great, but there is no way I could leave my cousin, I couldn't face the family. I told him, how about we bring him in and show him exactly what I just showed you. He agreed, brought his cousin to the next meeting (obviously there is a back story, he didn't share about getting his cousin to the meeting).

We showed the cousin a potential savings of $20,000, and he looked at the business owner cousin and said: "Why wouldn't you do this, it's $20,000!" At that point, the CPA cousin wanted to know what the process was, and how much time it would take. We went ahead and did the design of the plan for him and actually came back with a savings of $67,829 per year if he followed the plan. He almost immediately started implementing the plan.

This happens almost on a daily basis in our shop and not just with business owners but with individuals as well. Like I had mentioned before, if you don't get the taxes correct, nothing else really matters. After we got this client's tax plan in place, we were able to show him how he could create some tax-free income in retirement, reduce his health care costs in retirement, create a more tax-efficient portfolio and even develop a succession plan for the selling of his business. By showing him what is possible, we created a safe place (eliminating fear), created trust by giving him the free assessment (with a money back guarantee if we couldn't do what we said), and we did 75% of the work (lowering his time commitment).

What common misconceptions do your clients often believe to be true, but in your experience, are far from the truth?

Misconception #1 is - "I already have a guy who does this." Yes, you are correct you do have a guy who prepares your taxes. It is a common theme I hear day in and day out. The CPA you are using is doing tax preparation (and he is probably good at it), he is not being proactive and doing tax planning. You see tax planning is done all year long, not on April 15. If you wait until the year is over, we can't help you, it's too late.

A lot of the strategies that we use must be put in place before the end of the year, that would be proactive tax planning, not tax preparation. We do provide tax preparation as well, but the planning part is much more important. If all you want is someone to check off some boxes, then a preparer is all you need. However, if you want to keep more of what you make, then you need tax planning! Ask yourself this question, when was the last time your CPA or tax preparer came to you and said: "I have an idea to save you money?" My guess, never!

Misconception #2 is – "I have a 401k, and it is the best place to save for retirement." I agree that a 401k is a good part of a plan. If you have an employer match, it's free money, why wouldn't you? However, beyond that, is it really the best place to put money for retirement? We have all bought into this the concept of tax-deferred money now is much better than taxable now. We have been sold a bill of goods by large corporations and our own government. Again, a portion of the money, if you have matching should go into a 401k.

The IRS is just chomping at the bit for all of us to turn 70 ½ to start to receive all the tax money they missed out on during your working years. If you believe that you will pay fewer taxes later, then stuff all your money in tax-deferred accounts. However, with a country trillions of dollars in debt and a country that doesn't have any products to sell, how are we going to pay for the deficit? I'll give you a minute to think about it.... TAXES! Once you start taking your Required Minimum Distributions at 70 ½ you are going to get bumped up (not everyone, but most likely) into another income bracket, which in turns taxes more of your social security income, which in turn creates a larger cost for Medicare, which in turn leaves you with less money to live on, which in turn makes you take more money out of these accounts and it starts all over again. It is just a hamster wheel that you can't get off of. Find vehicles that you have control of, if it is tax-deferred, you do not have control of the distribution phase.

You have someone that is going to tell you when you have to take it, or else!

Misconception #3 is – "When I retire my health care will not cost as much." Well, that may or may not be true. It is really going to depend on when you retire, where you retire, and how much income you have in retirement. If you make too much money, as Medicare cost is determined by your Modified Adjusted Gross Income (MAGI), you are going to pay through the nose for health care. I run these projections using a software all the time for my clients. I had a family come in that makes a decent combined income, around $200,000 before taxes.

This client was 41, and his wife was 32. They have 4 children and want to keep the same amount of income they have today (it is a misconception that you will spend less in retirement, just saying), and they want to retire at 67. I won't get into all the numbers, but it is estimated, based on the income they want and a life expectancy to 90 that they will spend over $2 million dollars in health care costs! T is number does not even include long-term care costs in retirement. I don't know about you, but I thought saving $2 million for retirement, with Social Security, would get me through pretty easy, that barely covers health care. It is never too late to plan for this, find products that don't count as income against you in retirement.

What are some of the typical pitfalls your clients might not, but should be aware of?

Pitfall #1 is - Not having a plan. It has been said, "no one plans to fail, they just fail to plan." It is true when starting a business, a family, or even when it comes to finances. Again, if good tax planning is not done, nothing else will really matter financially. When a good sound financial plan is put in place, you will create a greater likelihood that you will be successful based on the plan.

Pitfall #2 is - Short-term thinking. A lot of times we cannot see 10, 20, or even 30 years down the road. We come from a world of the "I want it now" mentality. I see lots of people who have great cash flow but have nothing to show for it. They are out spending money on cars, going out for dinner, and exuberant vacations. In today's world, none of us want to wait and save for things, we would much rather go into debt and pay for them later. Eventually, this mentality catches up with you and can end up being a weight that you have to carry around with you all the time.

Pitfall #3 is - Not having a sound investment strategy. Most of us will look at past performance to determine if a particular company is doing well enough to invest in. The problem is most positions that do well in up markets may not do well in down markets. If you are looking at a particular company after 2008, it would be hard not to see a great 10-year performance. However, we could throw darts at a list during this Bull Run and make money.

Emotions can be a great thing, and they can be your worst enemy. As the market goes, we tend to become very emotional, buying at the high of a particular company and then selling at the bottom. We have to stick with an investment strategy and put our emotions to the side. It is very important to stick to a plan, which is long-term thinking, and gives a great sound investment strategy.

What common fears prevent your clients from even attempting to reduce their overall tax liabilities?

Common Fear #1 - The most common fear we face is trust. As I mentioned before, the financial industry does not have the best reputation for doing what's right for the client. Here we have tried to curb that fear by being a Fiduciary. A Fiduciary is bound by laws to do what is in the best interest of the client. By being an independent organization and a Fiduciary, we provide not only holistic planning, but we are very unbiased. We have no allegiance to any product, company, carrier, entity, or person. I like the ability to go out and find the best product or service for a particular client in a particular situation. Sometimes the products and services are similar, but in most cases, it is very individualized for each person who walks in the door.

Common Fear #2 - The second most common fear we have is the fear of change. Most of us are all procrastinators and really don't like change much at all. Think of how long you live in your home. The family will spend somewhere between 20-40 years in the same house. If we as humans enjoyed change, wouldn't we change our home, our state of residences, our jobs, or even our hair color much more frequently? We simply do not like change and will do everything in our power to avoid it.

Financial planning is no different. If you have a CPA or Financial Advisor, you have probably been with that person for a long time. Imagine if you have to go to one of these people and tell them you are switching services. We face that every day in our practice, and we help coach people through how to break up with their current professional. Sometimes, especially in the CPA space, we don't need to break up. Your current CPA may be a great fit if they play in the sandbox nicely.

It sounds obvious, but why would the people you serve want to work with a Financial Advisor?

For most of you reading this, ask yourself what affects me the most in my life? If you think long enough you will come up with one word, MONEY! When money is going well, our life feels amazing. However, when money is scarce, everything begins to suffer. I believe that the solutions really are not about the money that you can save from Uncle Sam or the money you could potentially grow your nest egg up to. The real answer is about how money is affecting your life. Having done this for over 15 years, it has never been about money, it is always what money does to your relationships, your health, your meaning in life, and your self-esteem.

Most of us will be in money struggles for most of our life, it is a common theme in our world. However, you don't have to be. Once you realize that money is the cause of most negative aspects of your life, you will begin to understand that this is a journey and not a sprint. When money is scarce, we argue more with our family. When money is scarce, we tend to work more, causing less sleep and our health suffers. When money is scarce, our ability to have a good self-esteem is diminished. When money is scarce, you begin to question everything about your meaning in life. Isn't time to take back control of your money and not let the money control you?

What led you to this field?

As a young farm kid, we learned hard work almost immediately after we could talk. I can remember my dad getting up at dawn and not seeing him until the darkness came over the farm. I can't remember a time growing up when my dad wasn't outside working. Whether it was during the day, in the evening, or the weekends, he was always doing something. With that hard work, always comes great responsibility. My dad may look at himself like this, but he was the first entrepreneur that I ever had known. Farmers normally don't look at themselves like that, they just go into the family business of farming.

Growing up on the farm had all of the advantages that most kids never get. I got to play outside every day and the playground at no limits. For as far as I could see, that was my playground. I was able to have recreational toys, like ATVs. I even knew how to drive by the age of 10. Most kids don't even know how to drive at 16. It was great growing up on the farm, a bit boring sometimes, but mostly great.

There was a moment when I decided to get into the financial services field. Like most farmers, my dad carried lots of debt. When you have to buy machinery, land, seed, fertilizer, and all the other miscellaneous items, you go into debt. My mother, bless her heart, loved to go into debt as well. As kids, we never went without.

I believe that is mostly how my mom accumulated debt. My parents, not unlike most, argued about money a lot. In 1988, we had a severe drought on the farm. My dad persevered, and we came out of that okay. However, a few years later we had another one of those severe droughts. Side note, if you think Las Vegas is a gamble, try farming and depending on Mother Nature.

This second drought would have sent us to the poor house, if not for my grandparents on both sides. The family helped, and we stayed in business. It was the first time I realized how important saving for rainy days and having a plan was in sustaining a lifestyle as well as taking care of your family. We didn't have any money in the bank, just a bunch of loans that needed to be paid. I also don't blame my dad for that, it is just what he knew, and no one taught him any different. My mom passed in 2004. She passed at the young age of 56, many years too early. I was already in the financial industry, as I wanted to help people like my family save for rainy days and tough times.

When my mom passed, it was another example of how they hadn't planned well, of course, they wouldn't listen to me. My mom had a life insurance policy of about $60,000.

That was pretty good planning on their part, except for the fact they had about $80,000 in credit card debt. Again, my dad persevered and got through this time, but how much easier would it had been if they just had someone that sat down with them and developed a plan.

Today, my dad lets me talk to him about financial stuff, but you know they never listen to their children, sorry dad. I do help him save money from our Great Uncle in Washington, but as far as making a plan, he uses someone else.

What are your final thoughts for high-income earners and business owners who want to reduce their overall tax liability, increase their profitability, and create and grow their wealth?

My final thoughts for someone wanting to develop a roadmap for their financial journey. Don't wait, if it isn't me, go see someone. It may take a little time out of your week, but it will be well worth your time. Most places will give you the initial appointment complimentary.

We are all procrastinators and believe we will get to it, but think about the things we always think we will get to. How often have you wanted to clean the garage, have a garage sale, call an old friend, or even send that letter to a dear friend? We never get around to it, because the world and time just move too fast. You can try going it alone, and if you do, that is better than not doing anything at all. You could also try and stitch up your arm instead of going to the ER, we know how that would end.

If the reader wants to know more, how can they connect with you?

If you like to learn more about me or my firm, Arseneau Advisory Group, visit our website at www.arseneauadvisory.com today for a complimentary no-obligation strategy session. In this session, your only obligation is to be open and honest about your current situation and where you would like your financial journey to take you.

If you would like to learn more about the retirement health care crisis in America, visit www.arseneauadvisory.com and get your free estimated health care costs in retirement report. You have nothing to lose and potentially everything to gain. Look for my upcoming books on the Retirement Savings Healthcare Crisis and The Business Owner Retirement Strategies.

LEONARD P. HAYDUCHOK

Certified Financial Planner™

Dedicated Financial Services LLC

Email: **Len@DedicatedFinancialServices.com**

Website: **www.DedicatedFinancialServices.com**

Call: **(609) 588-5353**

Len Hayduchok is a Certified Financial Planner™ practitioner and fee-based planner with more than 25 years of experience in the financial services profession. Len and his team of professionals at Dedicated Financial Services offer a full complement of comprehensive financial planning, tax preparation and investment advising services to meet their clients' retirement income, wealth creation, asset protection and legacy objectives.

Len is a graduate of the Wharton School of Business at the Ivy League University of Pennsylvania and earned a Master of Divinity degree from Biblical Theological Seminary. Len applies his education and experience in business and theology when advising clients how to integrate their finances to fulfill their highest life priorities. Len embraces his fiduciary responsibility to advise clients according to what is in their best interest as this obligation reflects his values.

Len enjoys sharing his knowledge as part of his commitment to client and community education, lecturing on extensive subject matter at local colleges, community centers and churches, and hosting a radio program titled Theology of Money. He has also published numerous resources on a wide range of topics of interest to retirees and those planning for retirement, as well as to younger families.

Len is extensively quoted in the financial news media including The Wall Street Journal, The New York Times, USA Today, Forbes, Newsweek, US News and World Report, CNBC, Fox News, and News12.

Describe the clients you work with and the types of situations they find themselves in when they come to you for your help?

I enjoy the diversity of the financial planning needs my clients bring to me. Everyone is in a unique financial situation and has a different view of the role money plays in their lives. Still, everyone wants their money to meet at least one of four common objectives: to feel financially secure, have more money to spend, be in financial control and feel good about themselves financially. It's interesting how almost everyone I meet thinks the solution to their financial objectives is "to have more money," regardless what their objectives are.

Sure, I work with my clients to grow their assets, but to me, as a financial planner, the key to my clients' financial success is making the money they already have more valuable to them--by aligning it with the things in life most important to them. At Dedicated Financial we use a wide range of planning tools and services to help our clients meet their financial objectives. We manage investments, create plans for retirement income, protect assets from every realistic financial risk, reduce taxes and file returns, and plan for the distribution of estates. This full-service financial approach allows our team to assist in some way virtually everyone we meet with, and to integrate all the individual pieces of their financial puzzle.

In order for me to help my clients maximize the financial potential of their money, they have to come to the realization that they don't know everything about every facet of financial planning, and working with a knowledgeable and trustworthy financial professional will help them realize their financial goals. This is especially true when they retire or go through life changes--retirement, health issues, loss of a loved one, what they want their assets to accomplish for them, and how much money they have. One of the things I find rewarding about my work is the close contact I have with my clients. It allows me to assist them throughout their lives, so they can enjoy life and don't have to worry about running out of money or going broke in a nursing home, and are protected from the many financial pitfalls that could ruin their quality of life.

What common obstacles prevent your clients from achieving their desired outcomes?

The individuals and couples I come across in my line of work are often their own worst financial enemies, and how they "do their finances" is their biggest obstacle. They could be in a better financial position if not for detrimental decisions they made or beneficial steps they failed to take. But it is particularly unfortunate when they're reluctant to change how they handle their finances when what they're doing just doesn't work.

There are those who know quite a bit about some aspects of finances but don't have sufficient expertise and experience in every financial discipline that could be beneficial to them. Their skills may have served them well--perhaps in managing their portfolios when the market was growing--but the limitation of their know-how can really hurt them if, say, the stock market should take a hit. Another shortcoming is thinking incorrectly that expertise in one area carriers over to other financial areas. Managing a portfolio for growth may not be the best strategy for retirement income planning; building wealth might be an ineffective solution for meeting long-term care needs; and accumulating a sizable estate might not result in an effective transfer of wealth to future generations. Sometimes individuals who know a fair amount are the most difficult to help because they think they know more than they do, or are intimidated by working with a financial advisor because it could make them feel inadequate. I want all my clients to know that I am on their side, helping them overcome their financial challenges when, if not before, they arise.

Another group of individuals who are their own worst enemy are those who are undisciplined or financially inexperienced. They tend to repeat the same pattern of poor financial decisions and can be unwilling to change how they handle money. These individuals can't foresee that their financial future will fall apart one day because things are "working for them" now. They need to know that the steady and predictable income stream they are enjoying while they are working or early in their retirement won't magically continue throughout their entire lives...and then what? They can also be careless with investment decisions and who they trust for financial advice by not asking enough questions about the financial recommendations offered to them and not researching the credentials and trustworthiness of the individuals they rely on for advice. I'm completely transparent with clients about how my firm works and make sure our clients understand the benefits and drawbacks of all their financial instruments, because there is no perfect financial product.

The last group of individuals who go about their finances in a harmful way are those who simply maintain the status quo, even when it will never get them the results they want. They are either accustomed to their current financial situation or afraid to make changes, and choose to be "stuck." These individuals may have difficulty trusting a reputable and knowledgeable financial advisor they come in contact with or may be reluctant to change a financial advisor they are currently using even if he or she is ineffective or does not have their best interest in mind. One client I have worked with for a few years comes to mind--a fellow in his late 60's who never married and never had children. "Tom" was soft-spoken and timid, and managed to accumulate sizable wealth, largely because he spent very little. The first time we met he was very guarded, but soon realized I wasn't trying to "sell him something." After a series of meetings I got to know "Tom" and understand him and his financial needs and concerns. Eventually he did some business with me, then progressively a little more as he felt more comfortable with me and knew he could trust me. I value "Tom" as a person and as a client, and we have developed a warm, cordial relationship as he has become confident with me and the services I'm able to offer him.

How do you go about helping your clients to avoid or overcome obstacles, so they can maximize the financial potential of their money?

Whether potential clients know a lot about finances, have been undisciplined in managing their money, or have been afraid to modify their financial picture, we have our clients set clear, straightforward objectives for what they want their money to accomplish for them, then build a plan to meet these objectives and regularly monitor our progress. This is a much different approach than simply investing money in a "well-diversified" portfolio and hoping that a certain amount of net worth will meet every financial need in the future.

Clients like how my Money Do List™ helps them understand what their Life Goals, Hopes and Dreams for their money are. Whether they want to spend money and enjoy a nice quality of life; have enough money readily accessible for emergencies and to have a financial cushion; see their wealth grow to a certain amount; and/or protect themselves from investment losses, catastrophic health problems, and other risks they can insure themselves against, the beauty of the Money Do List™ is my clients state their objectives in their terms. I don't redefine what they tell me they want with financial industry jargon (such as "long-term growth," "moderate risk" or "diversified portfolio") that has little meaning to them.

I take the Life Goals, Hopes and Dreams from their Money Do List™ and use my 5 Key$ to Financial Planning System™ to develop an Income Plan, Investment Plan, Tax Reduction Strategy, Risk Reduction Strategy and Legacy Plan which integrates all the financial planning disciplines necessary for them to achieve their financial success.

My financial approach gives clients assurance that their financial goals will be met just as we planned. Those who need to supplement their income needs with their portfolios feel confident that they will have money available to spend throughout their entire life; those who like security can sleep well knowing there is nothing to worry about because they have enough money in safe and readily accessible accounts; those who like structure feel in control because everything is in proper order and all their financial objectives have been addressed; and investors who like to see their wealth grow value the financial advantage of reducing the amount of risk they are taking to meet their growth objectives. Clients who work with me appreciate how easy it is to understand what I will do for them and how comfortable they are with my approach.

What common misconceptions do your clients have about using financial advisors to meet their financial planning needs?

To be honest, it can get a little annoying when consumers view financial advisors as a commodity, and don't value the superior set of skills, experience and expertise that the better financial advisors have worked hard to acquire. The key to getting good financial advice and putting it into practice isn't simply to "have a financial advisor" but to work with one who is well-suited to help you meet your specific financial planning needs. If you need a surgery, wouldn't you want to find the most highly qualified and experienced doctor, and if you need to be represented in court, shouldn't you look for the best attorney? Just like you don't want to use "any" surgeon or attorney, why would you settle for a financial advisor who is less than exceptional? When people tell me, "I have a financial advisor" I ask them how they know the advisor is doing a good job for them or, at a minimum, has the necessary qualifications and experience to help them meet their goals. Consumers rarely have objective standards to evaluate an advisor's capabilities. Instead, they make the mistake of relying solely on how "comfortable" they are with the advisor.

Some consumers I come in contact with are distrusting of all insurance agents and brokers, no matter how proficient and likeable they are, because they simply don't feel financial advisors are looking out for their best interest. They may be surprised to know that some advisors have special licensing and credentialing that makes them fiduciaries, meaning they are legally obligated to act in the best interest of a client. Certified Financial Planner™ practitioners as well as fee-based planners must place the interests of clients above their own in every financial transaction they recommend. I happen to be both. As a fiduciary my only consideration in making a recommendation is how the client will benefit; my personal financial gain is irrelevant. That's why my clients have come to trust me explicitly, do more business with me over time and eventually trust me to handle all their finances. And that's why they feel confident to refer their friends and family members to me.

Many of the folks I meet through my work have become cynical about the financial services profession, and feel that financial advisors don't care about them and just want to make money on them. Sadly, this sentiment is based on their observations and experiences with the financial services industry. Although you can never really know how concerned a financial advisor is, by getting to know the advisor and talking to other clients the advisor serves, you will get a good idea how much he or she really cares. I like to take my time when working with clients. I'm never in a hurry to do business with a client and never want anyone to feel pressured or rushed to make a decision about their money, which is an obvious red flag for advisors you need to stay away from.

When it comes to making the money they already have more valuable to them, what are some of the unknown pitfalls your clients might not, but should be aware of?

Consumers need to know to whom financial advisors owe their loyalty--is it to their clients or someone else? Financial advisors who work for brokerage firms have an "agent" relationship with their employer, which means their primary obligation is to act in the best interests of their employer. Financial advisors working for firms can be faced with a conflict of interest between making money for their employer and serving their clients' best interest which may be less profitable for their employers. This is one of the reasons I have chosen not to work for a large brokerage or another advisory firm--because I want to do what I know is best for my clients using the best products and strategies available in the market.

Consumers are shocked when I tell them how little experience is needed for a "financial advisor" to become licensed to sell financial products. The only requirement to sell insurance products is to pass a state exam after completing a 40 hour instructional program. Securities licensing also requires that an exam be passed, but for some licenses no instruction is required. Having such a low bar to get into the financial services profession is another reason why so many "advisors" give poor advice...they really don't have enough experience to know what they're doing. When identifying who to work with, consumers need to ask financial professionals how long they've been working in their profession, what alternatives may be available to meet their financial needs and what is the advisor's experience using these other strategies. They should also request and verify references and credentials.

Just like in any demanding profession, it takes a long time and a great deal of effort to master the necessary skills to be a truly qualified financial planner. I consider myself fortunate to have realized early in my career how important it is for me to be proficient in a wide array of financial disciplines and knowledgeable about the many financial products to serve my clients properly. Income and investment strategies, tax analyses, various insurances (life, disability, long-term care, and property and casualty), and legal documents (including trusts), must all be integrated to the specific needs of each client. Many consumers undermine their own financial success by not requiring the financial advisors they work with to provide the comprehensive service they need, which the financial advisor may lack the adequate training and expertise to deliver.

What fears do your clients have about even trying to have their assets aligned with the things in life most important to them?

Many people are concerned whether the financial programs they have in place will meet their needs for their entire lives or if they might run out of money one day. They worry that they may be spending too much or something catastrophic could happen and wipe out their wealth. Consumers may also have a nagging uneasiness that things just may not work out like they're hoping, accompanied with a feeling that their finances aren't set up quite right and they could be doing better for themselves.

At the same time people may either be "comfortable" or resigned to what they have in place and who they are working with, even if their financial programs and advisors are sub-par. The idea of making a change could be stressful to them, heightened by their most serious fear—getting ripped off. Folks have had bad experiences with insurance agents and stock brokers—or know people who have—and have become conditioned not to trust anyone when it comes to money...and I might add, rightly so!

Being afraid on the one hand that their money will fail to meet their needs and afraid on the other hand to change what they are doing, can paralyze people from doing anything. This is a shame because it won't allow them to get the better financial results they need. Consumers have to understand exactly what it is they want their finances to accomplish for them and get an accurate assessment of their financial situation. It will help them see if the strategies they have will meet their financial objectives, and if not, what corrective actions are needed. It is important that people have their financial position periodically reviewed by a reputable financial advisor they are not currently working with, similar to getting a "second opinion" after visiting a doctor who offers a medical diagnosis. Getting better financial results starts with being educated—knowing what you want and

184 | Remarkable Retirement: Volume 1

whether you are on the right path to get there. If not, how do you make the changes that will, and who can help you do this?

Change doesn't have to be intimidating as long as you clearly understand the process and objectives, and they're done at a comfortable pace. Change has to be a natural process where you discover whether a different course of action is needed and why. Take your time when making a decision to work with a new financial advisor. Check the integrity of the advisor and the firm you are considering with regulatory bodies and industry associations, know how the advisor gets paid and always be sure you fully understand the financial recommendations that are being offered.

It sounds obvious, but why would the people you serve want to maximize the financial potential of their money?

People want more out of life. They want their lives to be meaningful and to be passionate about what they do. They want their relationships to be fulfilling. They want to live life with no regrets. Although money is not the means to experience life to the fullest, financial means can promote a more satisfying and better quality of life...if assets are structured properly.

Too often folks settle for inferior financial solutions offered by less-than-fully-qualified advisors they "have a relationship with." As a result they deny themselves the full benefit of their financial wealth. Consumers need to place their interests above a relationship with their advisor, where they may actually be placing the interests of their advisor--to make money on them--ahead of theirs. I call this "misplaced loyalty" and always encourage clients and potential clients to do what is for them.

Consumers need to expect more from what their money can accomplish for them--more spending, more security, more wealth, and more control over their lives. And they need to expect more from the financial professionals they rely on for advice and service--better planning, better financial outcomes, better responsiveness and proactivity, a more comprehensive service, and a better overall client experience.

What led, or inspired you to work in the financial services field?

I started working in the financial services profession part-time while attending seminary full-time, preparing to be a missionary. Over time I came to understand that my workplace was my mission field--where I could help people structure their finances to achieve their Life Goals, Hopes and

Dreams in a way that is consistent with their spiritual values...if this was important to them. Most clients who choose to work with me see me as someone who is fully committed to helping them realize those things in life that matter most to them.

When I started the Dedicated family of companies in 2002, I selected the name "Dedicated" because it communicated my devotion to my clients but more importantly because it was my commitment to serve God through my vocation and reflect His values, love and concern for people. It's my privilege to serve the people I come in contact with everyday and to reflect God's goodness in my life.

What are your final thoughts for those who wanting to enjoy life, not have to worry about running out of money, and be protected from the many financial pitfalls that could ruin their quality of life?

The process for achieving a better financial outcome is actually quite easy: know what you want, assess if you're on track, make modifications as necessary and surround yourself with the financial professionals you need. You'll find that the actual steps aren't all that difficult either, once you decide that your financial future is important enough for you to take the necessary action.

Be "intentional" and disciplined with your money. Every financial product or strategy needs to get you closer to your goal. If your money isn't allocated appropriately, realign it with what's most important to you. Don't settle for inferior financial products and services that are convenient and profitable for financial professionals--it's their job to serve you! Remember, it's your money and should accomplish what you want.

Make your money as valuable to you as possible by structuring it to meet your Life Goals, Hopes and Dream, and in the process you'll "Bring Your Money to Life."

If the reader wants to know more, what's the easiest way to connect with you?

The easiest way for someone to learn about me and the work I do is to check out my website: www.DedicatedFinancialServices.com. There you can find out more about the services my firm offers, meet the members of the Dedicated team and access my educational resources.

Reach me by phone at 609-588-5353, or email me at Len@DedicatedFinancialServices.com to schedule a consultation.

During our meeting I will make sure you know exactly what it is you want your money to accomplish for you. I will also review your income needs, taxes, investments, insurance and asset protection strategies, as well as your estate planning preparedness to see if your assets are properly aligned with the things in life that are most important to you. The objective of our initial meeting is to get acquainted and decide if it would be beneficial to continue our discussion at a subsequent meeting when we would explore exactly how you may want me to assist you, and what solutions might be available. My team and I are always happy to point those who are not a fit for our practice in the right direction if we are not able to assist them ourselves.

We frequently offer educational programs to the public on a wide variety of topics related to financial planning and host client appreciation events where we get to know our clients better and meet friends and family members they would like to introduce to us. Some, but not all, of these programs are announced on our website, so it's better to call our office for a complete list.

RICHARD E. REYES, CFP®

The Financial Quarterback ™
Wealth & Business Planning Group, LLC

Email: **Richard@TheFinancialQB.com**
Website: **http://www.TheFinancialQB.com**
LinkedIn: **http://linkedin.com/in/thefinancialqb**
Facebook: **www.facebook.com/financialqb**
Twitter: **http://twitter.com/thefinancialqb**
Call: **(407) 622-6669**

I am Richard E. Reyes, CFP®, owner and President of Wealth & Business Planning Group, LLC (The Financial Quarterback ™). For over 18 years I have been exclusively providing Baby Boomer individuals and families with **sleep well at night solutions** to help them prepare and enjoy their retirement. In addition to running the day to day events in my practice, I love to teach. I serve as an adult education instructor throughout central Florida colleges where I teach courses on Retirement, Social Security, and Taxes.

I have been published and am a sought after avid contributor to various magazines, newspapers, and local television such as Fox 35, Wall Street Journal, BankRate.com, Orlando Business Journal, Bloomberg, and various others. I have also authored portions to the following books titled *The Dirty, Filthy Lies My Broker Taught Me and 101 Truths about Money and Investing, The Complete Guide to Investing in Annuities, The Mutual Funds Book* and most recently, *Remarkable Retirement.*

My success is driven by my clients' success – nothing is more rewarding than creating a successful plan for a client to help ease or eliminate their financial stress, worries, or fears. I love when clients retire, but most importantly, when they stay retired.

Describe the clients you work with and the types of situations they find themselves in when they come to you for your help?

I have built my practice since day one helping Baby Boomer pre-retired and newly retired individuals and families build *"sleep well at night"* solutions so that they could not only retire but most importantly, stay retired.

My clients are usually somewhere in their mid-50's to early 60's. There is a sense of urgency that happens during those ages. All of a sudden you finally realize that "long-term" that you hear so much about during your years of saving, doesn't seem that long anymore. You did a decent job putting money away, but life still got in the way a few times, markets fluctuated a lot more than you expected, or you come to the realization that you really had no clue what you were doing. You and your spouse begin to wonder how all these 401(k)'s, IRA's, stocks, bonds, pensions, social security, and those savings bonds in the shoe box go together. You Google the word **retirement** only to find that there are about 324,000,000 results dealing with the topic. It's overwhelming, and you have no idea where to start. That's when you typically reach out to me.

What common obstacles prevent your clients from achieving their intended retirement goals?

I wish I can say that there was only one obstacle people are faced with before they seek my help. That's usually not the case. They usually have a lot of concerns, some of them actually justified. However, these are not really obstacles. Most often they are just confused and find themselves not having any idea where to begin.

Google the word **retirement,** and you will get 324,000,000 results. The internet is an awesome tool that puts information at your fingertips 24/7. There is information overload, specifically, which one of those search results apply exactly to your specific situation and needs.

In addition, there is also another obstacle when trying to find information, which information is correct and who do you trust?

Advisor A says to invest everything in the market and take monthly distributions at a rate of x%

Advisor B says you should never invest your retirement in the market because you can lose it all. Remember 2008?

Then, Advisor C says that they have the answer that always works.

Then the radio host says the opposite of Advisors A, B, and C. Your neighbor says he does it this other way, and then let's not forget that Suze Orman and Dave Ramsey are plastered all over TV saying something totally different than everyone else, especially each other.

Which information to trust and from whom is something more and more people have a problem accepting.

This all leads to our natural state of anxiety, confusion, doubt, and fear. Fear will prevent you from making prudent decisions and stops you from being able to reach your intended retirement goals.

How have you helped clients to avoid or overcome those obstacles and to successfully achieve their retirement goals?

Educate, educate, and then educate a little more. From the very start, I have found that the topic of money and investments can be complex for many. We are never really taught much about the topic in school. What we know is often pieces of pieces of information shared among friends, families, and co-workers. So I have built relationships with my clients around educating them and providing answers and solutions that are specific to them, their individual concerns and objectives.

It all starts with our Retirement Planning courses at the local community college. I have been teaching there on and off for over 18 years. This gives them a simple foundation to start from. After class, I often meet with students to discuss their own individual objectives and concerns. I take a very straight talk and comprehensive approach to looking at their overall situation and building a plan. The industry concentrates on usually one issue; returns, returns, returns. I, on the other hand, don't. It's the simple "chicken or the egg" notion. If you have no idea what you are trying to accomplish and what you want your money to do for you, what difference do returns make? So it's important to understand what comes first. I have always found that if you skip all the steps necessary to build a comprehensive approach to your retirement and concentrate on which stock, bond, or mutual fund is going to give you the greatest return, you have just guaranteed your failure.

Even after we implement a retirement income plan for a client, it's not over. Consistent reviews to make sure we are following the plan is crucial. Life is not static. We don't live in a 3-ring binder or excel spreadsheet. Countless things such as death, disability, rough markets, bad health, job losses, and divorce happen to the best of us. In addition, there are also great things such as; an inheritance, bull markets, and even winning the lottery that happen as well.

So it's important to take the necessary course correction when needed to stay on-track.

Still, education is at the forefront of a relationship with our clients. Our multiple events, videos, newsletters, and blogs are provided in order for clients to remain educated and focused instead of worrying about what their friends or television is telling them.

Share some of the popular misconceptions that the people you serve may have about achieving their retirement goal?

There is a lot of misconceptions, sometimes even myths, when it comes to money, investing, taxes, and retirement. These myths and misconceptions about money and investing seem to be the same no matter who I'm working with. Upon closer inspection and our process, our clients are coached and better able to make informed decisions. If you do not become informed about these myths and misconceptions, they will work their way into destroying your retirement.

I think one of the most common misconceptions every person I meet believes is that there is some guru, investment manager, or stock picker that can consistently buy the best stocks and consistently beat the market. Here is the painful truth ... **No one knows who the hot stock-picking manager will be next - not even the mutual fund companies that hire them.** Why? Because there is zero correlation between a stock picker's market-beating performance and his ability to repeat that performance in the future.

Have you ever wondered why magazines only publish the "best" stock pickers over the last decade and never the future decades?

Additionally, retirement savers have been programmed that the success of your retirement is solely based on the size of your assets. They spend so much time in growing that pot of money that they totally miss, *"It's all about the income".* No one at the store cares how much money you have but rather, "Can you pay the bill?"

Retirement is not complicated, and there is only one (1) way to retire based on math and science. See the success of your retirement is really not about the size of your assets and this is a paradigm shift because your whole life you have been taught to save, save, save, and make that pile bigger. But assets can be lost, stolen, swindled, divorced, or decimated in a market crash or wiped out by long-term care.

The ultimate success of your retirement is based on how much guaranteed income you have. Unfortunately, investors, retirees, and financial advisors alike never understand this very simple necessary shift in mindset when it comes to your retirement.

The same is true when it comes to the topic of taxes. I often find that many don't understand taxes. This includes many CPA's, EA's, and Financial Advisors who are actually trained in the subject. I hear the following statement "I will pay a lot fewer taxes in retirement" so many times.

The amount of taxes you pay during retirement will be one of your highest expenses, if not the highest. Higher taxes mean less money for your retirement. The good news is that right now we are in the lowest tax rates in recent history. However, we have had federal tax rates exceeding 90% in the past. In fact, from 1936 to 1981, the top federal rate had never gone below 70%. Based on the current fiscal path, future tax rates will have to rise, or our country will go bankrupt. *It's math.*

Tax-deferred accounts like 401(k)'s, IRA's, Pensions, etc. are most commonly used by retirement savers. All these accounts have the same problem; **TAXES**!

The only real way to protect yourself from the impact of the eroding effects of taxes on your retirement is to work with an advisor who understands its impact and who will work with you to adopt a strategy to diversify your taxes in retirement. *Fewer taxes are always better.*

What common, but unknown pitfalls should the reader be aware of when considering their retirement options?

I work strictly with Baby Boomer pre-retired and newly retired individuals and families. I find there are common pitfalls with this group of people. If you don't have a plan to resolve some of these pitfalls, you will have a pretty rough retirement.

Most commonly people have no idea how long retirement is becoming. Not accounting for longevity is a major problem. Not only for yourself, but also for your spouse.

When I first started in the business 70 was considered old. But I now see more and more people living well into their 90's. Some of my own clients are now in their late 80's to early 90's, and they are extremely healthy. People are living longer than ever before.

Longevity is not only a major risk but a "risk multiplier." The longer you live, the longer you have to deal with all the other inherent risks during retirement. I.e., inflation, market returns, income, deflation, healthcare, etc.

Another big problem is that once people have a good idea about how much money they have, they are not quite sure what to expect from it and how to use it. How much you withdraw to sustain your lifestyle plays a key role. I find many who are just withdrawing too much.

The bottom line is that the longer you live or the more you withdraw early on in your retirement, the greater the risk of depleting your savings. Pair that with poor investment performance, and you have a problem.

Most people have no idea how easy it is to run out of money during retirement.

Additionally, many people think their health insurance or Medicare or some government program will pay for their long-term care. The truth is they don't. The financial burden can be devastating.

No retirement plan is complete without a plan for long-term care. *Not having a plan* **WILL COMPLETELY WIPE YOU OUT!**

What do the pre-retired and newly retired individuals and families you work with fear the most about working with financial advisors?

You must admit you are an addict in order to cure your addiction, right? Well, the same is true for many people in dealing with their investments, retirement, etc. The financial industry and advisors have gone through various transformations. Just like an addict who knows they need help, people know they need help but have little idea of what a really good financial advisor does, where to find them, or even what questions to ask. Even when they do hire a financial advisor, some won't even follow their guidance.

Often, it's not really that they are fearful, but they are making up an excuse. People don't want to be told they are doing something wrong. People don't enjoy being told their investments stink. People are also often embarrassed by their past and life mistakes. So, what often is fear it's actually just an excuse for them to continue running from the problem.

"I can't afford you" is a common excuse.

Here's the interesting part of this excuse; you are already paying for advice. No one is investing for free. If you look inside your 401(k), IRA's, or any other accounts you will notice that someone is getting paid for providing that service to you. After you account for the value provided from hiring the right Advisor in the form of planning, tax planning and preparation, low-cost asset allocation and portfolio management, estate planning, and maintaining peace of mind for you and your spouse, the cost is insignificant.

Another excuse I hear is "I don't have enough money to hire an Advisor."

No need to worry since Financial Advisors come in all "shapes and sizes." It's true that there are plenty of Financial Advisors, Brokers, and Banks that cater to a very exclusive clientele, however, more often than not we don't. I do not have any minimums. I have always felt that my role is to serve and help my client. If the client is serious about working with an Advisor, then I will be serious and work with them.

But the best excuse is "My Friend went to a Financial Advisor who lost all their money."

I am not going to tell you that this never happens but the instances are rare. There are many ways to protect your hard-earned money by asking a few simple questions. In addition, understand that having a relationship with a great financial advisor is a long-term relationship. Take your time and interview them. There are lots of us out there. Find the one you understand and can work with the best.

There are various sources to learn how to interview a financial advisor. My website has a very useful FREE REPORT which will allow you to learn some basic questions and the appropriate answers to them. You can get it by linking http://thefinancialqb.com/download-9-critical-questions. You can also check their background and a host of other information online. Our industry is highly regulated, and the information is easy to find.

It sounds obvious, but why would the people you serve want to achieve this outcome?

Many investors believe that a Financial Advisor's role is to pick a couple of mutual funds, fancy them with market jargon, and then spew worthless geopolitical and economic babble about why your investments didn't work and why you need to sell those old mutual funds and buy these new ones. The cycle repeats itself over and over.

A good Financial Advisor is much more than that. They will work together with you and look beyond just your investments in order to incorporate a holistic approach that includes tax planning, retirement saving and spending advice, estate planning, behavioral coaching, education, and much, much more.

It's easy to Google a specific topic and read the information online. It's more complicated to put all the pieces of information relating to your financial challenges together to meet your specific needs.

The value you receive from working with a good financial advisor goes beyond the traditional planning aspect and encompasses your whole life. It will definitely allow you to **Sleep Well at Night.**

What led you to this field?

Many in the industry didn't really start here. It's only through some of life's twists and turns and looking for a way to make a living that many become Financial Advisors. If you have a passion for helping people, then it's a great job.

For me, I always knew that I wanted to work in this field. My dad passed away at an early age, and my Mom was faced with making multiple financial decisions. We all know that the topic of money and investing is difficult today even with the vast amount of information in our hands. Back then, there were fewer options available. Watching my Mom struggling to navigate her way through many financial decisions gave me the desire to enter this career to help others.

After college, I didn't go straight into the field but kept it in back of my mind. It wasn't until one day that I was helping a coworker put together his retirement plan, and he recommended that I become a Financial Advisor because of how patient and knowledgeable I was in helping him sort through his own financial plan. This co-worker actually became my first client when I went into business.

What final thoughts would you like to share with someone who not only wants to retire but most importantly, stay retired?

My final thoughts are that ANYONE can achieve a *"Sleep Well at Night"* retirement. You just have to be willing to seek out the right Financial Advisor and be able to be open and truthful with them. You also have to be willing to listen and build a long-term relationship with them.

A great retirement is achievable through Persistence, Patience, and Planning.

If the reader wants to know more, how can they connect with you?

Our mission as **YOUR** advisor is to provide a personalized plan and process which will allow **YOU** to sleep well at night

We focus on **YOU**. We are **YOUR** financial planner, investment advisor, and coach. We are strikingly different to what you're used to from the usual providers of financial advice. Our loyal clients seem to agree.

We take the time to develop a complete understanding of **YOUR** individual circumstances, financial goals, investment objectives, concerns, and aspirations. With that information, we can help YOU make smart investment decisions while keeping **YOU** focused on **YOUR** intended path towards a secure retirement. We work with **YOU** to help **YOU** grow and protect **YOUR** wealth with cost efficiency and reliability.

What we are **NOT**:

- We are **NOT** stockbrokers!

- We are **NOT** commissioned salespeople!

- We are **NOT** annuity and life insurance agents!

- We do **NOT** have fancy offices downtown overlooking the city.

- We do **NOT** run big TV or Radio ad campaigns nor do we sponsor major sporting events.

Are YOU ready to see how The Financial Quarterback™ can help? ***NO RISK, NO HASSLES, NO SALES***. Simply contact me at (407) 622-6669.

Mention this book and your initial planning fee will be only **$375**. That's an outrageous discount. My clients pay between $1,100 and $1,800 for me to prepare their "***Sleep Well at Night Retirement Inspection***" plan. The best part, I am only charging you **$375** for the same plan.

That is right! ***ONLY $375***. No shortcuts, no less work, no less time spent with me.

RICK AIKEN

President & Founder

Wealth & Retirement Advisors, LLC

Email: **raiken@wradvisorsllc.com**

Website: **www.wradvisorsllc.com**

LinkedIn: **www.linkedin.com/in/rickaiken**

Call: **(704) 926-7555** - Fax: **(704) 910-4652**

Since 2003 we have been educating clients through multiple forums: wealth & retirement workshops, radio shows, adult education courses, federal benefits workshops, social media and client appreciation events. Our commitment is to enlighten you about complex financial concepts in easy to understand language.

Over the years, we have helped people from all walks of life grow and protect their life's savings, reduce or eliminate taxes, help send their children to college and create an Income for Life, that is in many cases, *Tax Free.*

We currently represent clients from the Washington, DC area all the way to Puerto Rico. My team has over 50 years of experience in all aspects of Wealth & Retirement Planning. We also share Strategic Partnerships with CPA's, Certified Financial Planners, Attorneys and Estate Planning Firms to craft a comprehensive Financial Blueprint, just for you.

Rick's radio show on 730AM ESPN Charlotte, *"Safe Money Wealth",* has been impacted countless lives and is available on his website or download upon request. Look for the new book "Remarkable Retirement" in the Fall of 2017, in which Rick is a contributing author. His insights will enlighten readers on a powerful, yet little known financial strategy.

Describe the clients you work with and the types of situations they find themselves in when they come to you for your help?

We help people from all walks of life, at many different stages of life when we first meet, and craft for them a Financial Blueprint that will be the financial foundation for the rest of their lives. What does that mean, specifically?

Let me share a story with you that almost all of my clients have heard: There is a very successful psychologist, Dennis Waitley, who was also early in his life a Blue Angel pilot in the space program at NASA. Dennis has worked with very successful people the world over, from Olympic athletes and CEO's, to survivors from the concentration camps in World War II. He shares what they all have in common, what vital tool they use that we all possess to realize their dreams. I first heard Dennis tell this story many years ago and it was so enlightening, so powerful, that it still resonates and guides me to this day.

Here it is: At NASA, when they are building a rocket to go into outer space, into orbit to circle the earth and then return safely, NASA is painstaking about the creation of the foundation of that rocket, and its launch. Everything must be just right in that foundation and that rocket so that when it launches, it does so without blowing up, and heads to its destination is space. Now, an unimaginable amount of time and effort goes into making sure that the rocket is well built, prepared to withstand all the challenges of going into space and back. For the rocket, *a lifetime*.

But, that is just the first step, granted a *HUGE* 1st step to achieving its goal of getting where it wants to go, which is outer space, to complete its mission and return *safely*. The rest of the way something else just as important must occur, because, according to NASA that rocket will be off course 98% of the time. <u>And that rocket, like your *mind*, is *teleological*, or *target seeking*</u>. It's a psychological fact. And so, NASA is constantly adjusting the course of the rocket to get it to space and back. And they have done this repeatedly in the space program with unbelievable, *predictable* success.

Why am I telling you this? Because when we craft your Financial Blueprint, regardless of where you are in life or how old you are, we too are painstaking to make sure of these two things:

1. We will get your foundation right, ready to launch, so you'll realize the life of *your* dreams

2. We will constantly fine-tune your financial course to make sure your life's journey and destinations are the

ones you've envisioned, providing you with peace of mind all along the way.

We work diligently on behalf of our clients to craft the financial rocket ship *they* want, and continue to "tweak" their financial course, so they realize and live the life of their dreams, worry free.

What common obstacles prevent your clients from achieving peace of mind in their retirement years?

Misinformation - When you Google the word "Financial" you'll get several million listings. That alone is enough to make your efforts to find out what you need to know to make an informed decision daunting. Add to that, the fact that those who dispense "just information" like Suze Orman or Dave Ramsey, know this: they are not held to the same standard as a licensed practitioner. They do not have the same disclosure rules and laws to abide by as those who are licensed, professional practitioners. They are not subject to criminal prosecution because they are not licensed and not facilitating the acquisition of any financial instrument. I believe they mean well, but as they are not licensed and directly facilitate the acquisition of all the financial products in the market, they are always speaking in general terms, with a very broad brush. As a result, they tell people their opinion without having first hand, accurate knowledge of what they are speaking. In many cases, their "advice" is completely inaccurate.

Procrastination - Let's say you do navigate the volumes of information with clarity, which are loaded with landmines that can undermine your efforts to build *your rocket ship*. And now, you have what you need to make an informed decision, but you just *cannot*. <u>*Procrastination*</u> has ruined many a good person's effort. Kept them from capitalizing on many wonderful things in life. In their efforts to know all there is to know, so they don't make a mistake, they make the biggest mistake of all, they do *nothing!*

I've been there, about half my life ago. On the verge of letting my efforts to not make a mistake, to want to have everything perfect before I could take action, cost me what at the time was the greatest opportunity of my professional life. Fortunately for me, I had a trusted advisor, a man who became my mentor at the outset of my career to consult with. I called him, as I was agonizing over my decision. I'd already been offered the position, my first on the national stage. He had now relocated back to the west coast, I on the east. I said, "Pat here is the situation, and I started to go in great detail, as he had always stressed that I do my homework. After about 5 minutes he stopped me. He said: "Rick, have you done your homework, really been thorough? I knew I had and replied yes. He then said: "Go over one last time the pros & cons of this opportunity. Then, let it sit overnight. When you wake up tomorrow, ask yourself one final time, "Do I take this opportunity?" And then make your decision confidently".

And here is what he said next, that I still hear in my head like it was yesterday: "Because, Rick my boy, know this: "*If you look hard enough and long enough at anything, you'll find something wrong with everything.*" My first real bout with severe procrastination, fearful of making the wrong choice. I have relied on his wisdom and this simple approach to everything in life and shared this pearl from my mentor more times than I can count. It always works.

How do you help your clients to avoid or overcome the obstacles that prevent them from achieving peace of mind in their retirement?

We craft their Financial Blueprint or Rocket Ship, specifically for *them*. In almost every client assessment, we have discovered a *void* in their current plan, *if they even have one*. This Financial Instrument is not in their plan, and, *they usually know little or nothing about it*. This is amazing, because one of the key provisions of this strategy and the vehicle to achieve it, has been a part of the tax code longer than the 401k statute. And deferred tax umbrellas like 401k's, TSP's and 403b's to name a few, are exactly where the vast majority of Americans save the largest amount of their money for retirement. Now, it's true that when you are offered the match by your employer, the first thing you must do is contribute up to the matched amount, so your employer will match you up to their maximum. It's free money, you must take it.

Now, here's where the story changes. Most folks have money in savings accounts, money markets, cd's, stocks, bonds and mutual funds. They may have some income producing rental properties as well. Some have college savings plans like a 529 or educational IRA's. But, upon close examination, almost all of them, even the most savvy, do not have the vehicle & strategy I've referenced above and which I'm about to tell you.

Here are the main benefits our clients realize:

A. Stock Market Losses are Eliminated

B. Opportunity for double-digit interest earned annually, (this has happened in some strategies 20 of the last 30 years)

C. Eliminates All Future Taxes to create a Tax-Free Wealth and Retirement Fund

D. Access to your funds at any time with *no* penalties or taxes

E. Creates a Lifetime Income stream 100 % *Tax-Free*

F. And, though treated tax-wise like a Roth IRA or Roth 401k, you can contribute amounts *much greater* than the Roth limits, in the $10's to $100's of thousands of dollars *every year.*

G. And a few more that are very valuable, to be addressed at a later time.

What is the Financial strategy and instrument that provides these benefits, that most people don't have in their Financial plan or don't even know about? It's a properly structured cash value life insurance strategy, using an **Indexed Universal Life Insurance contract.**

What common myths or misconceptions do your clients have surrounding their retirement goals?

They do not understand this strategy - With *rare* exceptions, when I first meet and talk with people and business owners the first challenge is they've not heard of this strategy or the vehicle that helps them achieve the benefits I listed above.

And though this is not a new idea, something that is already proven over many, many years and can withstand close scrutiny, most folks *just don't know about it*. We will enlighten you on all the pros and cons of this strategy so you can make a fully informed decision that is in *your* best interests.

They believe it will cost too much - At some point on the path to learning fully how this strategy will work for them, the question is raised: I've heard this is expensive, my investment advisor (who is not licensed to facilitate the acquisition of an Indexed Universal Life Policy) and therefore does not have access to, or the knowledge of all the inner workings of this vehicle, says so. Or my banker or another life insurance practitioner, all of whom do *not* have access to this product category.

Unfortunately, those who decide to just accept this feedback without getting all the facts from an unbiased, qualified practitioner are making decisions based on limited or inaccurate information. Most likely, they're missing out on a very powerful addition to their financial blueprint. <u>Because the facts are these</u>: When compared to all other financial vehicles and analyzed impartially, the costs are comparable. When viewed through the *net* financial gains lens, in many cases, our clients do better financially. Factor in the *tax savings*, and this *outperforms any other single financial instrument, with no risk of losing money in the stock market.*

It's too good to be true - Now, on the surface of things this may have some merit, and I hear this from time to time. I sometimes hear this too: Everybody I talk to says not to do this. When I ask who "they" are, I hear all sorts of things: My investment advisor, my family, siblings, friends, their doctor, lawyer, plumber, very smart friends in other professional walks of life. I'm sure they're all well-meaning. However, they are not dedicated professionals in this field and do not have the knowledge or insights into all the factors they must consider.

Here is your reality: Be sure to obtain clear, unbiased, factual information, where all aspects of this approach, all the pro's & cons of including it in your Financial Blueprint have been addressed with you by a reputable, licensed financial professional. Then you can make an informed decision, with peace of mind, knowing you have been diligent and confident in the outcome you are seeking, *with predictability*. There's also another saying we hear all the time, which is based in fact: That "Contempt prior to investigation is Ignorance." No one wants to act or make these life-changing decisions in this frame of mind. And you do not have to.

What are some of the unknown pitfalls or mistakes that the reader might not, but should be aware of?

First, at heart and in reality, some people are do-it-yourselfers. They approach all issues in life believing and acting on information that just they gather and assess. They may be a professional engineer for example and a very gifted one. (I'm not picking on engineers here, they could have any vocation or come from any station in life) Because of their belief in themselves and the success in another field, they believe that if they do their own diligence and make decisions based on their findings only, they'll get the best outcome.

They believe they'll eliminate bias, weed out the unqualified and surely know that someone else's best interest, like a qualified financial advisers, are not placed ahead of their own. Unfortunately, because they are not licensed practitioners, the likelihood that they will create a comprehensive financial plan, where all the parts complement each other to serve *all* their needs, does not happen. And they end up vulnerable.

Second, they do not fully comprehend, "The Big Picture". To truly make thorough, thoughtful decisions on anything in life requires *"Big Picture"* thinking. It's the old "ankle bones' connected to the shin bone, the shin bones' connected to the knee, to the hip, etc." Today we hear the term, *unintended consequences* a lot. Either way, a multitude of issues exist from the time you enter your career until you retire, hopefully continuing to live the life of your dreams. These variables appear and become front and center in your life at different stages and ages. Those will be the ones we know about. That is challenging to be sure. Then, add in the ones we do not. Those we don't see coming. A 9/11 catastrophe or the collapse of the financial and housing markets in 2008 and you have some serious consequences to navigate. Can you afford another few years of stock market losses like those that occurred in 2008? Where the S&P 500 lost over 40% of its value in *less* than 60 days? Where, factoring in inflation, the 2008 levels of the stock market were not realized again until 2016? If you'd had a balanced Financial Blueprint, one with *"Big Picture"* thinking in place before these events occurred, the impact on you financially would have been *reduced* or in some cases, *eliminated*.

And third, be sure you are working with an *unbiased, holistic advisor.* One who practices to the *fiduciary standard.* Which is: to always place their client's interests ahead of their own, to best serve *them.* This will require that your practitioner has the ability to offer all financial instruments, whether investment or insurance based. An advisor who works with professionals in all the areas that will affect them:

legal, tax, health, estate and financial. Because, the impact of improper planning will magnify the impact of *unintended consequences*.

What common fears do your clients have about even trying to achieve their retirement goals?

One is the *fear of not getting what you want*. In the financial world, most people exhibit this fear by refusing to maintain a proper asset allocation between risk or market-based products and insurance or safe products. They believe that when the markets are experiencing record highs, that this will always be the case. They may tell us differently, but when it comes time to adjust their risk, they refuse to take action. *This fear is the fear of thinking they will miss out on making more money, through market gains, <u>or not getting what they want.</u>*

The second fear is the *fear of losing what you already have*. In this scenario, people are so fearful of risk that they place all their life's savings in safe or insured products like savings & money market accounts, treasury's, cd's and sometimes bonds. They believe that these products cannot lose money, not always true in the case of bonds, and by earning much less than the inflation rate over the last 35 years, about 3% annually. The result is that they will not have enough money to carry them through retirement without reducing their standard of living or running out of money.

Third, and *by far the number one* fear when asked, people say that when it comes to retirement, their biggest fear is running out of money before they die. In a day and age where pensions have almost disappeared, and with the future and access to Social Security changing and uncertain, making sure you won't outlive your money is a real and viable threat to your financial security. If this critical component is not built into your financial blueprint, where you *know* what your retirement income stream will be, and that you *cannot outlive* it, then there are 2 real dangers you will face: First you may well have to lower your standard of living, perhaps significantly, or secondly, there is a possibility that you may maintain that standard, only you'll run out of money. Neither of these are acceptable options to anyone we have served over the years.

Why would your clients want peace of mind and less worry about their money running out during their retirement?

First, when thoroughly examined, if this strategy *does fit* into your financial blueprint, the benefits to you and your family or business will or may include: predictability, reduced stress, enhanced financial growth, increased levels of total liquidity and a huge reduction or elimination of *all* future taxes. Which means you get to keep significantly more of what you've worked so diligently to earn and save.

To achieve this, we need to be able to enlighten you with what you *need to hear, not necessarily what you want to hear.* Having these conversations, addressed with candor and compassion are essential for your well-being. If you are seeking more peace of mind, less worry about your money or how your financial life will unfold to live the life of your dreams, then engaging with us may be right for you.

What's your backstory, what led you to the financial services field?

I did not plan to be here, like many other respected professionals I know, they came from successful careers in other industries. In many cases, like mine, their industries shrank for many reasons, leaving a lot of talent to find a way to utilize their skills and successes in new arenas. At the urging of peers, friends, and colleagues, I finally looked at the financial services industry. Concluding that I might be bored to tears in this business, I entered anyway. In the first 2-3 years, I thought my assessment was becoming a reality, and I was not finding the growth and passion for my work I had enjoyed and thrived on for the first 20 years of my career.

Then, one day, I was attending senior-level meetings with an affiliate company. Different educational topics were being presented, all providing snippets I needed to know to best serve my clients and stay abreast of best practices. But, nothing I would not have learned in another forum in a timely manner.

After lunch, a woman took to the front of the room and began to enlighten us on a financial strategy & vehicle that was new to me. This included the platform to achieve the benefits she was describing. The longer she talked and wrote on that whiteboard, the more intrigued I became, I actually felt my passion *ignite!* When I left, I began to learn all I could about was she shared with us. After that day, I *knew* I could help people and business owners. I felt *inspired* again, something that professionally I was beginning to wonder if I'd *ever* feel again. And today, I feel and *know*, more strongly than ever, that what happened that day still inspires me to help people live the life of their dreams. We make that our client's reality.

If the reader wants to know more, how can they connect with you?

We welcome the opportunity to be of service. We offer a no cost, no obligation one-hour consultation. When we meet, our purpose will be to learn more about each other and see whether we'll be a good fit to work together. We know we cannot help everyone, for many different reasons. If that's the case, we'll be candid and let you know so that so we don't waste your time, or ours either. No one wants to be the "round peg in the square hole," and we respect that your time is just as valuable as ours.

To request your free consultation or learn more about us, visit our website: www.advisors llc.com. There you will see just a few of our Client's Impressions of their relationships with us and have access to my 730AM ESPN Charlotte Radio Show: *"Safe Money Wealth."* You may contact me through the website, email me directly @ raiken@wradvisorsllc.com or call me at 704-927-7555 to schedule your consultation. We hope the life of your dreams becomes your reality. Because as we believe, "It's not *just* about your money, it's about your *life!*

NICK SLOANE, CHFC, CRC

Chartered Financial Consultant
& Certified Retirement Counselor
President, Sloane Wealth Management

Email: **nick@SloaneWealthManagement.com**
Website: **www.SloaneWealthManagement.com**
Call: **(630) 529-0199**

Nick Sloane is President of Sloane Wealth Management and has been an outstanding financial services professional for over thirty years. He is certified by the American College in Bryn Mawr, Pennsylvania as a Chartered Financial Consultant (ChFC®) and has received the Certified Retirement Counselor (CRC®) designation by the International Foundation for Retirement Education. He acts as a fiduciary Investment Adviser Representative of SGL Financial, LLC, and a Registered Investment Adviser.

His has been featured in such publications as *The Chicago Tribune, U.S. News & World Report, The Daily Herald, Investors Business Daily, Fiduciary News, Yahoo Finance* and others.

Nick takes a holistic approach in working with clients to help create the retirement plan best suited to them. He helps them avoid any threat of running out of money during their lifetimes; makes sure they can pay for health care and long-term care costs; as well as reduce unnecessary risk with investments. He also ensures their estate planning is up to date, helps them find ways to reduce taxes and much more.

Nick considers that things will change, not only with the personal lives of his clients, but also how the financial world innovates or moves in different directions.

Describe the clients you work with and the types of situations they find themselves in when they come to you for your help.

Although I don't have an exact minimum or maximum, I generally assist middle to upper-middle-class individuals and couples with liquid assets upwards of $300,000 to $5 million.

People come to see me because they have many concerns about how to plan for retirement. They ask such questions as:

How do we know we have enough money to retire?

Others are:

How are we going to pay for health care costs in retirement?

Should we allocate our money differently?

Are we on the right track?

When should we take Social Security?

How do we make sure we don't run out of money?

Are there some things we don't even know about that should be of concern to us?

How do we create enough income to support us in our retirement?

What do we do about inflation?

How can we reduce our taxes?

Standing behind these concerns is the very real worry about how long they can maintain their standard of living after they stop working.

A survey done a few years ago showed that most people have a greater fear of running out of money than dying! This makes a lot of sense, since running out of money does represent a sort of "living death" -- as your money starts to "expire," so does your lifestyle.

I show my clients the various ways in which they can build a foundation of safety around their assets so they will be able to cover their spending needs and at the same time, greatly reduce their risk of outliving savings.

What are some common obstacles that prevent people you meet with from achieving their goals in retirement?

There are many and they are mostly about our behavior. On the one hand, many people have done a lot of things right; they've saved, put the kids through college, didn't live beyond their means and so forth.

On the other hand, when it comes to how they will handle finances to better support a retirement, there are some behavior changes to consider and making changes can be quite difficult for them.

Procrastination, overconfidence, tunnel vision and short-term thinking are just a few. I can also add that many people miscalculate how rates of returns might not work in a way they think they will or should.

At the most fundamental level, it is a person's lack of understanding what a comprehensive retirement plan really looks like or how to develop one that will best serve their goals.

Procrastination starts with the many considerations people ought to explore about their retirement planning. Frequently, they don't quite know where to get started so there can be some inertia involved.

They may not be sure where to turn to get some personal guidance. Perhaps they don't even realize how they could benefit from getting professional assistance in planning for their retirement.

Even when there is some interest, it can be difficult to quantify how an advisor could help if you have never worked with one. There may be concerns about being taken advantage of as well, which can justifiably give people cold feet. I think it is understandable why so many people avoid taking the plunge and hiring an advisor; or, getting a new one.

Misinformation is also rampant and makes for plenty of confusion. A lot of what we consider doing with our money often comes from long-held assumptions, many of which might not be completely accurate.

Information that people buy into or take for granted can be obsolete or can come from the wrong places or from people who have an agenda, which is frequently designed to benefit them and not so much you.

This is especially true when it comes to financial advice you can find on the Internet.

Being too confident also has its perils. This is happening now because there is a lot of focus on recent financial history along with the growth of investments.

Many people are feeling quite happy at this moment, as the stock market has been doing well for a few years. They say to themselves "We have a great guy handling our money," or "I am feeling terrific about how well I have been able to recover from the crash."

Yes, we have seen double-digit stock market returns over the past several years. However, there is a kind of an amnesia about the more distant past, which colors how people might see the present or especially their future.

For example, the average compound growth rate in the S&P 500 Index from 2000-2016 was less than 3%. On top of that, the average rate of inflation was about 2.8%. The net increase was .2%, in other words.

But, many people might shrug their shoulders at facts like these. They might say, "I don't think I've done that bad." If so, it might be that they - like you, have been contributing to a 401(k). These contributions offset the impact of losses, at least to a degree.

Regular deposits into savings provided the illusion of suffering fewer losses. Of course, bonds did better and some global indexes, too. But, for most people there was (and still is) too much of an emphasis on larger U.S. stocks.

They also might feel that since "the market always comes back", there is little to fret about. It's okay to wait. Unfortunately, this attitude might not serve their interests, particularly after they retire.

In fact, if you look at that S&P history, the recovery from market crash took seven years! If you add inflation, it took longer than that.

What really matters is this: it's not how much money you have or how well the market has done for a few years, it is knowing how much you can safely spend over a long period - and what can affect those expectations. You also must figure out how much you can afford to lose at any given time.

In short, you need to think about your money in a different way, especially when you require a plan that needs to support you for 30 years or more.

And, there are several other important factors to consider besides the growth of your savings. If not addressed, these too, could have a very negative effect on the quality of your retirement.

What I have also found is that most people believe they already have a retirement strategy. They think their 401k, IRA's, brokerage accounts, savings, social security and a pension are what constitutes a plan. What they have are *some* of the ingredients, but not a plan itself.

It's kind of like trying to build a car with parts from different manufacturers; say, a drive shaft from a Ford Focus, an engine from a Volkswagen Passat, a steering column from a Toyota RAV 4, on a chassis by Hyundai.

You get the picture. Maybe the car will run, but how well and how reliable will it be?

Similarly, a piecemeal approach to savings and then creating an income plan for retirement might also work. On the other hand, will it be the best, most efficient way to help you live a happy, healthy and secure life during your retirement?

I do think everyone should be more open to new or different ideas. This is not an easy thing for most of us, especially around finances; and, I am sympathetic to that. But, I truly believe it's necessary to accept that the financial world has changed. Otherwise, it becomes pretty hard to create an up-to-date, comprehensive retirement plan.

How have you helped your clients avoid or overcome these obstacles to successfully achieve their goal of having a great retirement?

The solution to not running out of money or not feeling more secure about your retirement is to have a good plan, with some flexibility to go along with it. However, you must also know where to start. Otherwise, to quote the famous baseball player, Yogi Berra: "If you don't know where you're going, you might wind up someplace else!"

When I meet with people, we have a conversation about their current lifestyle, their vision for their retirement, and the steps they have taken to date. It's usually clear to me when folks don't have their ducks in a row.

Nonetheless, it isn't what I think that counts, it's what they think. If I feel there are problems to address and people are open to a deeper discussion, my goal is to support them in seeing their issues more clearly.

Starting to question traditional ideas about money and retirement is part of that conversation.

For example, the conventional wisdom says you need to produce say, 80% of your pre-retirement salary after you stop working to meet your income needs. Or, you should have at least ten times your prior, annualized income in savings. I always wondered where exactly did those rules come from or who made them up?

Everyone's situation is different. Some of you might only need 50% of your annual salary after you leave your job, while others might need 100%, as an example.

Financial planning includes knowing what a realistic investment return looks like and deciding what rate of inflation should be used. What are your expectations of future tax rates and how will Social Security and pensions fit into the picture? How do you ensure enough income if you live until you are 90 or even 100 years old?

These are just some of the questions that need to be thought through, which means you also have quite a few decisions to make.

To me, having greater financial security entails making the best possible use of good information and that you choose a professional you can trust. Otherwise, confusion can inhibit your decision-making. As someone in my business once said, "We help people free themselves from the tyranny of having too many choices."

At the end of the day, it can be very difficult for you to get helpful knowledge from your family, acquaintances or online that is accurate or the best for _your_ situation.

But, many of the pitfalls of retirement can be minimized with proper planning. How you arrange your finances right _now_ can limit potential future losses, help you be better prepared to pay for expenses and really start to allow you to feel that your retirement will be the best it can be.

What are some common myths or misconceptions that people may have about achieving their goals?

One myth is that many people assume the old money "rules" from 20 years ago still apply today. For example, there is something called the "4% rule," which says you can take out 4% of your investments each year, then annually increase those withdrawals for inflation and have a high probability of not running out of money during retirement.

A problem with this is called the "Sequence of Returns Risk." This ties into the issue of average returns and how many of us miscalculate.

The 4% rule can lead you to assume that if you only take out less than your average return in the stock market, you will be in good shape. If your average is 6%, well by golly, pulling out 4% or 5% should be okay, right?

The answer is…. not really. Stock market volatility can make buying into that rule a gamble.

To be specific, it's NOT the average of your returns that matters; it's the order of those returns. If you suffer a downturn in the market early in your retirement, the thought that you can still take increasing income from investments as you wait for a full recovery is probably not going to turn out very well.

It might help to think of a couple of examples, such as the three years in a row the market dropped from 2000-2002, or just before 2008.

Instead of having your income last for 30-35 years, a poor sequence of returns might cause your savings to last only as little as half that time.... or perhaps even less than that.

Of course, if there is a positive early market return after you retire, then taking all your income from investments could certainly work in your favor.

Your assumptions about where the stock market will go - especially in the first few years of your retirement, will play a significant role in how you plan for long term income. But, as Clint Eastwood once said in a movie: "Are you feeling lucky?"

Another misconception is having unrealistic expectations of high investment returns in the future. I often hear prospective clients say they expect to get 8-10% returns in stocks or mutual funds without taking on too much risk.

Long term average returns in the future may well be considerably less than the past, according to several institutional research sources, unless you really want to up the ante in terms of risk.

This notion can be hard for a lot of folks to fathom, given the steady market growth over the last several years. However, it's also a reason why you need to take the long-term view when it comes to managing risk.

In situations like this, I ask my clients a straightforward question; one that they have likely never been asked or asked of themselves: "How far are you willing to see your investments drop to get the return you want?" In other words, "How much are you willing to lose?" This can get us back to a more realistic and therefore, useful conversation about investing during retirement.

Avoiding a lot of buying and selling to "beat the market" is also a better way to lower risk for most people. This activity simply does not work over an extended period, either for individuals or even for most professional money managers.

This is one reason Warren Buffett says if you cannot hold a stock for ten years, don't hold it for ten minutes.

Also, many people who come into my office tell me they believe they are well-diversified, when this is usually not the case. Besides allowing for longer holding periods, it comes down to how broadly allocated your investments are, too. Allocation and time are two proven factors to reduce your investment risk while also increasing the potential for good, consistent returns.

I should add that the fees you pay really do matter. It's not just an outside management fee that can affect your bottom line, it's also the costs inside your funds.

You can pay a higher management fee with one advisor and still wind up paying less in total expenses compared to an advisor whose management fee is lower. The first one uses super low-cost funds while the other puts you into investments with higher internal expenses.

I use an objective research method that shows my clients how well their asset allocations stack up and how much they might be overpaying in total fees. This includes expenses that are hidden from the average investor's eyes.

The report they receive also demonstrates what their investment returns could look like moving forward, assuming things are left as they are now. People are frequently surprised when I share their evaluations with them.

What are some of the pitfalls to being able to maintain your lifestyle in retirement?

Here are just a few:

Longevity risk. People are living to be far older than they were a generation or two ago. Today, if you take a typical 65-year-old couple, one of them has a 50% chance of living to 92 and a 25% chance of living to age 97. Case in point: although my father passed away at 91, my mother turned 97 in February 2017. In my planning process, I tell my clients they need to prepare to live to at least age 95, even if they think otherwise.

Market risk. As I already discussed, the bull run of the 80's and 90's and especially the current run up over the past several years, has given many people a renewed sense that the market is doing fine and will remain predictable.

As a result, they have returned to the complacency of the 1990's. I am not alone in believing long-term volatility is probable and the Sequence of Returns Risk is something to consider. Hedging your bets on the roller coaster of stock market volatility might be a wise move for a lot people.

Inflation risk. We have lived for quite some time with low overall inflation. However, costs that will affect retirees more than other people include things like health care and the price volatility of commodities such as gas or food. According to many economists, just the rising cost of health care alone could be extremely burdensome.

Social Security benefits might not increase that much in the future and will certainly not keep pace with the already high cost of health care. Also, most private pensions don't go up with inflation.

The bottom line is a lot of experts in my business think people who want to properly prepare should assume that overall inflation will be *significantly* higher over a long-term retirement.

Taxes. Believe it or not, many people could wind up paying more in taxes during retirement than for health care. This includes ALL taxes, such as property taxes and sales taxes, not just income taxes.

For example, with your 401k or IRA, you must take a Required Minimum Distribution - or RMD, for short - after your age 70 and one-half and then report it on your tax return as ordinary income. An unpleasant consequence might be that your Social Security benefits then become taxable, with the result of seeing a big jump in your income tax rate. All by simply having to take your RMD.

Of course, I'm also sure you are as aware as I am, of the many reasons why taxes will probably rise in the future. The deficit, the pressures on funding Medicare, Medicaid and Social Security, not to mention state budgetary shortfalls; are all just a few examples and any one of these problems will count heavily toward that probability.

Health Care and Long-Term-Care Risks. According to a Fidelity report, the average 65-year-old couple will spend well over $250,000 for unreimbursed health care costs during retirement and this only accounts for people living into their mid-80's.

It also does _NOT_ include the cost of long-term care. A long-term disability could easily wipe out your savings. Not only will this be financially devastating for you but it can also financially and emotionally devastate the lives of your loved ones. There are some ways to reduce your financial exposure and _they do not necessarily require that you buy insurance_.

Unfortunately, few people are planning for this high probability event. They often do not think a disability will happen to them or they have thrown their hands up in the air and given up thinking about it.

Personally, I believe it is an advisor's duty to be persistent with clients so they don't wind up shooting themselves in the foot by ignoring this problem or any of the other ones I've mentioned.

The bottom line is that any of these pitfalls can subject you to what is called an "excess withdrawals risk." This means due to unforeseen circumstances (such as underestimating inflation), you now must increase the percentage you must take from savings just to pay your bills.

Month after month goes by and you suddenly wake up and realize the value of your investments is slipping away -- significantly.

How would this make you feel? How might this affect your lifestyle, your relationships or even your overall health due to stress? There may be some good strategies to fix these problems, if you are willing to consider them.

What do the most common fears people have when attempting to get their retirement plans in order?

I think the number one fear that prevents people from improving their financial situation goes back to the issue of trust. Often, they don't trust themselves. I say this because of how shaken up so many people were after the 2008 crash. They felt they were doing everything right and they still lost a ton of money.

As a result, most people don't want to make mistakes, which is perfectly understandable.

They worry that making changes could lead to more trouble, even though it doesn't necessarily serve their interests to leave things as they are. Therefore, it can feel less risky to stay put, mainly because it's familiar.

So even when there is pain associated with your current situation and you know there's something missing, you might feel torn about what to do.

As I mentioned earlier, what's clear is that the financial world has changed and this world is far more unpredictable and complex than 20 years ago. You don't want to wait and figure out how to fix the dike after it begins to break apart and spill its contents. Instead, I believe the better solution is to check for weak spots early on and repair them in advance of a potential disaster.

It sounds obvious, but why would the people you serve want to have outside help, or use a different advisor to help them create a lasting plan for their retirement?

I truly believe one of the most important things is for people to understand how their emotions will affect their retirement planning, for better or worse. Thus, a good advisor needs to help clients see how their instincts might not be serving them well.

Research has shown that it's a person's emotion-based behavior that makes the biggest impact on the quality of their retirement. Literally, emotions make it to the decision-making part of our brains faster than rational thought processes.

From my perspective, the ultimate reason for having a plan is to feel more secure that your money will last as long you do. That's really the bottom line and is why people can do some good things and not so good things with their money. In part, they are searching for "shelter from the storm," to quote Bob Dylan.

Our behavior isn't really based on numbers or computer simulations that are supposed to predict likely outcomes. After all, I am sure you are familiar with the phrase "past performance is not indicative of future results." Most of us want to know we can do more than survive, we want to thrive, financially and emotionally.

If you think about it, the major reason why government workers, teachers and those with sizable company pensions are the happiest people in retirement is that they know they have a license to spend. A large chunk of their income comes from a fully predictable source.

Meanwhile, many of the people who have the greatest amount of savings are often the most tight-fisted because they greatly fear a slide in their investment accounts as they continue to take more and more money out. And, if there is a downturn in the market at some point, it will naturally compound their anxiety.

The bottom line is that we all want more freedom to do the activities we enjoy. Money is just fuel for the journey and it's really all about the quality of your life!

I cannot tell you how many people I have worked with who wind up with a palpable look of relief once we have implemented a plan together. They have finally nailed down something that is simple to understand and allows them to have more certainty around their retirement.

They also realize they can get a good rate of return and are confident a market drop won't have them panic. And, they know they have a "go-to" person who is going to be there for them over the long haul.

I think these are some great reasons to get outside help – especially from the right type of advisor.

How did your career in financial services develop?

When I began my career over 30 years ago, I was interested in how to make people's money work better for them. In my first decade or so, I primarily served my peer group, as well as business owners and professionals.

When my grandmother fell ill and my mother could no longer take care of her, I suddenly learned how people in retirement who haven't preplanned can really suffer financially and emotionally.

That is when I started moving in the direction of working with those who were nearing or were early into their retirement. I felt there was a huge void in people having a plan for a more secure future.

As someone who is also interested in human behavior, I learned not to just focus on numbers; but also learned I needed to help my clients feel better about their retirement prospects.

I also came to understand that using investments alone or just focusing on growth does not mean you have a real plan for retirement. My eyes were especially opened to all this back in 2008.

What are your final thoughts for the reader who is considering working with an advisor or perhaps changing to a new one?

Naturally, my final thoughts for those who want to ensure that their retirement will be successful is they consider working with a financial professional who is both a retirement income specialist and is truly a holistic advisor.

Too many people in my business are primarily interested in just managing your investments or they attempt to solve your problems by only using market-based products.

Unfortunately, there's also a common, yet understandable perception by the public that people like me are all the same.

In addition, they frequently believe most advisors are more concerned with themselves and the client's needs always come second.

Therefore, after the crash I chose to take on the responsibility - and the liability, of becoming a fiduciary planner. Although I always knew I put my clients' interests first, becoming a fiduciary meant that I now had the _legal obligation_ to do so. I felt this would give my prospective clients a more comfortable place to start when choosing to work with me.

I further believe you should work with an advisor who is independent and unbiased; who can help you look at allocations both within and outside of the stock market. This is very important as many types of products have potential benefits.

Every client of mine is unique and how we plan to use their assets to reach their goals can be quite different from what others I work with choose to do. I always thoroughly discuss the advantages and disadvantages of each aspect of a design process. This is something I think everyone should expect from any advisor.

If those I work with are committed to improving their situation, I am also happy to move forward at a pace that suits them. My approach is always thoughtful and supportive, as I understand how difficult making changes can be for some people.

My goal is to help people like you achieve the best retirement possible and make sure you can sleep well at night, no matter what financial storm passes through your life.

I believe I'm a very different type of advisor than you might expect or have experienced from the past. I have a unique approach to retirement planning; one that is comprehensive, is as unbiased as possible and where my clients' interests always come first.

If you are interested in talking with an advisor who meets these criteria, my invitation is to have a visit with me and see if we could be fit to work together.

An initial visit works like this: you just bring yourselves in and all we do is have a conversation. If we both think it makes sense to meet again, we will go from there. No matter what - even if we don't decide to work together, my goal is to help you to better help yourself. It's really that simple.

If the reader wants to know more, what are some ways that they can connect with you?

I would like to offer you a few opportunities to see more of how I work. First, I will gladly provide you with the report I mentioned regarding your investments. This is an objective review of how well your money is performing in the stock market relative to fees and allocations. It shows you ways to improve your diversification and reveals ALL the fees you are paying, including the hidden ones. To put it in more basic terms, it tells you if you're "getting your bang for the buck" with your investments.

Also, you can attend one of my seminars as a way of getting to know me better. Please use this link: www.SloaneWealthManagment.com/events and if you find a program of interest, you can email me directly at nick@SloaneWealthManagement.com or call me at 630-529-0199 so we can save some room for you. On my website, you can review other reports and information such as financial research studies and relevant articles that you might find useful. And of course, I am more than happy to offer you a complimentary consultation at a mutually convenient time.

Investment Advisory Services are offered through SGL Financial, LLC, a SEC registered investment adviser. Insurance products and services are offered independently through individually licensed and appointed agents.

PAUL ROTH

Senior Broker, Freedom Brokers

Email: **paul@freedom-brokers.com**
Website: **www.freedom-brokers.com**
LinkedIn: **www.linkedin.com/in/paulrobertroth**
Facebook: **www.facebook.com/diabeticinsure**
Twitter: **@PaulRothinsure**
Cell: **(618) 922-2105**

Paul grew up in the Midwest. After his father lost a job during a recession, Paul transplanted to the hardscrabble Mexican border of Texas at the age of 18. Taking summer jobs in the deep South Texas cotton gins, he graduated with honors from University of North Texas.

After graduation, working in Dallas in the medical software field, his life changed overnight when his mother was struck with cancer. Paul moved back South Texas to work his father's small business while his mother recovered. Years later, a new venture drew him to Marion, Illinois, where he lives with his wife Angelica.

Paul has firsthand experience of the struggles of small business, and the suddenness of life's changes. Married since the 80's, his life revolves around sports and family. A state champion in three different sports, his proudest accomplishment is winning first place of a "How Well Do You Know Your Daughter" contest on a Father-Daughter Night.

Who is your ideal client, who do you help?

My clients typically describe themselves as "Middle of the Road." Grab a piece of paper and pencil. Draw a line and write the numbers on a scale of one to ten. A "one" has no financial savings or knowledge. A "ten" is entirely set for generations. Circle the number that best describes you and your retirement situation. Where on the scale would you say that you are?

If you circled a one or two, you likely do not need my services, and I wish you the best of luck.

On the other hand, if you are a nine or ten, you also do not need any help. Pat yourself on the back, splurge on a nice bottle of champagne to celebrate your retirement and your great-grandchildren's inheritance. If you are really a ten, the drinks are on you.

However, if you rated yourself a three to an eight, are starting to think about retirement say, age 50-70 Congratulations! You have worked hard, saved some money, Yes, you made a few investing mistakes. (One of the most successful Wall Street traders I know made a million bad trades.) Yes, there were challenges, life experiences, and setbacks. Together, you worked through them and should be proud of what you have accomplished. You came out with more than you started.

The day will come when you step out the door for the last time. You put down your tools, whether they be a hammer and saw, or a stylus and iPad. You will have no more paychecks. Retirement is a totally uncharted territory and can be a bit scary. Unless you want to live the golden years with no idea of your spending limits, investment strategy or planning for the unexpected, you have a new challenge. To sleep well at night, you need to generate a clear roadmap of what must be done to have the income to last a lifetime. Let's work together until you have a clear plan for the future. Take a deep breath...

My wife likes flowers. Every year, like clockwork, she goes to the nursery to purchase those small pots of flowers. She does a great job, and the splash of color make the yard look stunning. I, on the other hand, like planting trees and shrubs. Maybe I am lazy, but I like my work to grow, and not do the same thing over year after year. When the weekend of the flower planting arrived, I went with my wife to the local garden center.

There was one sharp landscaper there, and you could tell he knew his stuff. He had dirt under the fingernails, cracked calluses, and a bit of silver in the hair. Work shirts that had been worked in. There he patiently answered the incessant questions about petunias, geraniums and every other flower imaginable. My turn came. I asked the question, "What's the best time to plant a tree?" The simple answer came. "Ten years ago."

We put off many of the most important decisions in our lives. Why? You are reading this book because retirement looms, and is calling to you. The best time to create a plan is ten years ago. Since we have no DeLorean time machine like in the movie "Back to the Future" you need to start now.

In my meetings with clients, when we peel back the layers of the onion, procrastination to establish a retirement plan and creating a perpetual retirement income machine often comes from underestimating or overestimating their lives and abilities.

If you underestimate your abilities, remember that life is not a dress rehearsal. You have gotten this far, and if you can plan a wedding or a vacation, you can, with some help, plan your retirement. Know that you will likely have to rethink some of your prior decisions. You may have to fire an underperforming advisor, even if he is your uncle. You may move some money around, change some of your investments, move some risk money to save money. You have to have the confidence in your plan to make the adjustments necessary to get the job done. Action is required for change. You can do it.

Overestimating your abilities is a sure fire way to fail. Remember the joke: *Do you know a redneck's last words? "Hey y'all, watch this!"* Trying to do too much outside your budgets or resources is the path to financial ruin. You may be the best science teacher in the world, but chasing the next penny stock or investing in the guru that promises fantastic returns is not the thing to do. We all think that we are immune to scams and downturns, yet remember how painful it was to live through 2008 or see fortunes fly away nightly on "American Greed" on CNBC.

Take a 360-degree view of your circumstances. Remember when your mom told you how to cross a street? You had to "look both ways." If you are looking only back and realize the mistakes you made, and are using old information to make those decisions, you will not succeed. Likewise, if you only look forward, and not making use of your experience, successes, and failures, you are also likely not to succeed. You've gotten this far, and with some professional help, can make the leap to a comfortable retirement.

Finally, be honest and open with each other and your advisor. Henry and Bess had been married for 60 years. To stay together for that long, you have to be completely honest with your partner. So Henry and Bess were very open, shared everything and didn't have any secrets from each other. Well, almost.

Bess kept a shoe box in the closet, which she had asked Henry not to open or even ask about. Henry never thought about the box in 60 years, until the day Bess got very sick. The doctor said she wouldn't make it. While trying to sort out their affairs, Henry took the shoebox to Bess's bedside, and she agreed it was time for him to see what was inside. Henry's eyes widened as he discovered $95,000 and two crocheted dolls in the box.

"When we were to be married," Bess explained, "my grandmother told me the secret of a happy marriage was to never argue. She told me that if I ever got angry with you, I should just keep quiet and crochet a doll."

Henry was deeply touched, two dolls meant she was angry with him only twice in 60 years!

"Honey," he said after overcoming the emotions "that explains the doll, but what about all of this money? Where did it come from?"

"Oh, that?" Bess said. "That's the money I made from selling the dolls."

How do you know who to listen to?

Is a personality on the television or radio right because they have developed star status?

Who is more right, Jim Cramer or Suze Orman? Do any of these celebrities actually come up with a plan for you? Do they know your risk tolerance, liquidity, goals, and dreams? Likely not, unless you are their first cousin. For your answers, you need to be guided by someone who takes the time to listen to you. Whether next door or across the world, find someone who understands you and can help you.

An acquaintance, Vicky, has very curly hair. She has been going to the same stylist for several years now. She likes the stylist, goes to her church, but the haircuts look like Homer Simpson meets Phyllis Diller. Vicky has taken magazine photos and shown them to her stylist. I asked her why she does not change stylists, and her response was something like, "How can I do that? She expects me to come every Tuesday. What am I going to say?"

Poor performance from a friend is no help to your retirement. Once you have made the commitment to implement change, how do you find the right advisor? In your first meeting with a potential advisor, discuss the elephant in the room. What is that element? Trust. When you have that queasy feeling, become focused. Problems or concerns should be brought out front and center. Do not go forward until you are comfortable, and listen to your instincts. Ask some tough questions. Make the commitment to get the "trust thing" out of the way before you waste any more of your precious time or any more of the potential advisor. Don't pretend to like someone, or try to be nice. If you and your advisor can't see eye to eye, or if you are getting a financial "haircut" it is time to get a new advisor. Once trust is established, go with the process.

I have released clients in the same manner. They just didn't feel right for me. Some advisors and some clients pretend. Not all clients are willing to divulge their finances. That is certainly their right, just as it is my right to reject the client if I don't think it is a good fit. Only armed with the proper information and trust, am I able to step back in a way and use my tools and skills in a way that the client can't.

Face the facts, be as objective as possible, and ask as many questions as you need to. Become comfortable with the solution. Be prepared. If you would like to get a checklist of questions to ask an advisor, send an email with the heading "advisor checklist" to returnonassets@hotmail.com and I will send it out free of charge.

Phil and Donna Hue came to me with their broker's statement and wondered why they were not progressing as well as they had hoped. When we peeled off the layers of expenses, (some listed, and some hidden fees) the Hue family was being charged about 4% annually! In an average stock market year of 7%, the broker took over half. Ouch! And worse yet, on a down year, the numbers got worse, and they lost all the gains they made in a bad year. Had they only called earlier, they could have saved some heartache. So ask questions.

I am happy to report that the Hues are now paying have been reduced, some money has been placed in low risk, low expense, tax-deferred products, and their retirement is back on track.

Had Phil and Donna properly vetted their advisor and gotten past the elephant in the room? Did they ask for and get answers to the advisor list of questions earlier they could have had no down years, and risked little or nothing of their retirement.

New clients often have misconceptions about financial planning. I have the rule of Six P's "Proper Prior Planning Prevents Poor Performance." So, whether you plan or not you will get an outcome. If you do not plan, your outcome will reflect it.

Good advice is not free, whether you get it from your doctor or your financial advisor. On the other hand, if I am only getting checked for a cold, I don't want to be charged for a heart transplant. What is really expensive is bad investing and making mistakes late in life with too little time to recover. Some of the low volatility and low-risk products in which you can invest have lifetime commissions far less than one-tenth of one percent.

The most successful plans are easy to follow and easy to understand. I advise my clients to use a bucket approach to placing your money. Your money is allocated among different buckets, each bucket represents the needs and methods of creating the income for that five-year period.

A common, but often expensive misconception is that Wall Street stockbrokers are required to look out for your best interest. No such requirement exists. Stockbrokers are paid to sell stocks. No more, no less. Stockbrokers are held to a "suitability" standard. If you can afford it, the sale is suitable. Let me explain. Betsy, a friend of ours, loved to be the center of attention.

When she was in her 20's her low cut blouses and short skirts made quite a stir in the neighborhood. Now that she is in her 60's, like many of us, gravity has let her north go a bit south, and Betsy packed on a few extra pounds. Selling her a shiny clingy pink sequined sweater in this meaning of the word, is "suitable" for her, as it does fully cover her upper body. She will not go to jail while wearing the sweater. However, it may not be in her best interest to be wearing something that might break if she breathes.

A fiduciary is held to a higher standard, always having to do the right thing for the client. A fiduciary standard would require that the salesman offer Betsy something more "age appropriate" and size appropriate. Look for an advisor who acts as a "fiduciary".

My college degree was recreational therapy, with an emphasis on psychiatric therapy. I worked with patients who ranged from major league ballplayers to union workers. We all have problems, and there are caring and competent people out there to help.

One of the most interesting cases was a brilliant man in his mid-forties who had a thriving legal practice in Florida. The only problem was that he had never gone to law school or passed the bar. When he was barred from the courtroom, he chose the medical profession and became a practicing surgeon, well respected. Unfortunately, he never went to medical school or passed the boards.

How was this brilliant man caught? He miscalculated the amount of local anesthesia needed to perform his own vasectomy and had to call 911. Brilliant mind, but not using the right professionals.

Another pitfall is using an advisor you can't fire. There was a very successful jewelry store chain my friend Brian worked for. If you ever asked the owners the secrets to their success, they would always say, "Don't hire your relatives. I can fire my employees, but I can't fire my brother-in-law." To this day, in over 30 years in the insurance business have never sold a product to a relative other than to cover my wife and daughter. I like to be able to fire my clients too.

There are always new laws and rules coming from the government. Most are well-intentioned and designed to protect the consumer. However, I have heard some twisting of the new Department of Labor rules that are designed to squeeze out the last drop of commissions.

From one of my clients, the conversation from the stockbroker went like this, "We now have to charge you <u>more</u> because of the new rule. It makes us have to tell you what we are going to charge, and since we have to tell you, we will have an additional fee to comply." Holy cow!

So how does one find the right advisor?

When I was first out of college, I made a commitment not to get married for a year. I wanted to make sure that the woman I married was truly the one I wanted. The only way I could figure that out was to find out what I didn't want. So for that year, I went out with women outside my comfort zone. Maybe I dated a woman a little older. Maybe she had more freckles than I was used to. I even tried a few zanier than my norm. Yes, I had some bad dates. But that didn't keep me from finding out what I did need in my life.

Hiring an advisor is much like finding a wife. To do it right, you divulge financial secrets and dreams, explore a lifetime of successes and failures. When you hire me, I am bound to you to help you succeed. So if that first advisor was not the right one, find one that works for you.

A common fear among my new clients is that that "You don't know my personal situation" Back in the 1980s I owned a mobile home sales lot. I had Bobby Lee, a very experienced guy working for me in doing the normal repairs, setups, and make ready necessary in that business. Often he would have a customer, not knowing his experience level, ask him, "Have you ever seen this before?" Well, every home only has one or two bathrooms, a kitchen, and some bedrooms. They are put together by nails and glue. After twenty years or so, yes, you've seen it. His standard answer was, "no ma'am/sir, but I read the book on the way over." His humorous way of saying yes brought a smile and a sense of confidence to my customers.

While I may not know your personal situation, we are all forgetful, wonderful, loving, jealous, secretive, exasperating, thoughtful, passionate human beings. I have advised clients with sick children, ailing parents, recent bankruptcies, old money, new money, close to death, and with newborns. I have a general game plan that makes financial sense. We vary the game plan, but not the game, from client to client,

Look at two facts. The market has created millionaires. Money in the market is at risk. At retirement age, not all of your portfolio needs to be at risk. Stock markets have performed well over a long historical period, but if you were heavily invested in 2008 and wanted to retire in 2009, you would have been a world of hurt. Some of those folks are still wearing red vests and checking out groceries. Sometimes we get burned badly enough trying something to not want to do it anymore.

This is true with financial issues. Unfortunately, we make the mistake of going totally in the opposite direction. I have seen some investors who, after a bad investment, will purchase nothing but a bank CD, thinking they are "Risk-Free". What they fail to understand is that time is also a risk. If your CD investments are making "zero point bupkiss" and inflation is taking away 3% of your earning power each year, you are losing 3% a year to time.

Earlier in the chapter, we discussed the concept of buckets and the influence of time on the buckets. The closer you are to retirement, the more you need to look at investments with little or no downside risk that gives you a greater margin of safety. Put more money in the safety bucket. If you follow the bucket method, you will properly fund your retirement.

There is an old FM radio station in all of our heads, WIII-FM. The station isn't rock, country or classical, but listening to that station late at night is a recipe for no sleep. WII-FM stands for "What's in it for me?" What is my outcome going to be? It's the radio station that plays late into the night. It creeps into your subconscious, and it does not let you sleep.

And it only plays one tune "Am I going to outlive my retirement?"

How do you turn off that noise in your head?

You could do nothing. Probably not a good idea.

You could Google. Many of my clients say, "I'm not good with money." I had a meeting with a potential client who took their life savings, googled "investment professionals" and gave their savings to a large brokerage house and never open up the statements until he came to my office.

You could procrastinate. One of my dad's best golfing and buddies, (and an incredible pilot) John, dated a woman named Liz. When I say dated, they dated for 15 years. He never popped "the question." He was 40 when they got married.

My most successful clients commit to making a solid plan with me. Let's do the work - once - and then sleep well. The only action will make the late-night sweats go away. Soon after the wedding, my dad and John went golfing. Dad took out his Spalding "Johnny Potts" Signature clubs out of our garage and put them in the back of John's red 1961 Chrysler Imperial. John's Imperial was replete with white seats, huge fins, fancy horn. Dad asked him, "How's married life?" John replied with a huge grin on his face "Why did I wait so long?" Make an accurate assessment of where you are now, and where you need to go. Then create a "Perpetual Retirement Income Machine." I can show you how.

After the work comes a great night of sleep. Have some of the fun you always dreamed about. Months later, John sent out a birth announcement to all his friends. "7 lb. 4 oz. redhead was born" - It was an Irish Setter. Once you have a Perpetual Retirement Income Machine, have all the fun you want!

Most times, when people meet, we are asked what we did for a living. I am often asked what led me to this field.

The mystery of finance and investing has been in my blood. My first job was as a paperboy. I went door to door to collect and got lots of coins as payment. In 1964, when coins changed from silver to copper clad quarters and dimes, I kept some of the silver coins, and still have them. My first stock pick was AT&T. I was 12 at the time, and under a federal Gifts to Minors Act. I still have that certificate also.

One of the jobs my father had was as an officer in the trust department at a local bank prior to the recession. He would bring home stories of children fighting over an inheritance. He would fret over the lack of planning on some people's behalf.

His pearls of wisdom were often at the dinner table and expressed in exasperation. His frustrations made me want to make sure I had a roof over my head when the storms blew.

I bought my first house right out of college at 22, on an FHA plan that allowed me to put sweat equity into the house for my down payment.

As a serial entrepreneur, I have been in the mobile home business, used car business, custom home building business, and a printer toner recycling business. Some worked out better than others. Never having the luxury of a pension or retirement plan, all the mistakes and successes are my own.

The price of education is far less than the cost of failure. I took finance courses for several years at the local college. I had some success at trading and volunteered to be the president of the college investment club. During my tenure as president, I was honored to pick the brains of nationally known celebrities like Jon Najarian of CNBC, founder of Trademonster, and author/speaker Toni Turner during their backstage time.

As I took a more advisory role in my other business interests, I completed the career change from business owner to financial advisor.

Some final thoughts for the reader who is committed to improving your retirement:

Truthfully assess where you are now. A goal without a date is a dream. Doing what you have done before has gotten you to that number on the financial scale of 1 to 10. Are you sleeping well at night? If you want to move up that financial scale, you have to make changes.

Take the time to plan - NOW. When it the best time to plant that tree? Twenty years ago. Life passes us by so quickly.

Take the time NOW to plan your retirement. Netflix, your grandkids, and your life will be there after you finish. In reality, it takes an average of four to eight hours of committed time to make the plan for you.

Still not convinced that it would work for you? Remember the story earlier of Bobby Lee? There are hundreds of behind the scenes players with thousands of years of experience behind each and every case. I have access to some of the best minds in the business.

With your honest self-appraisal and the advisor's proper questions, a "Perpetual Income Money Machine" (PIMM) can be created for just you. What is a "Perpetual Income Money Machine"? A system based on those buckets we described earlier. A system is a plan in action. Once your turn on the PIMM that you create, you will sleep well at night, knowing that your PIMM will pay you for life. I can help you create that "Perpetual Income Money Machine."

I love stories, listening to them, telling them, and learning from them. We'll laugh, perhaps cry. I love the imperfections of life. I am one of them. I am irreverent at times, financially pull no punches, but promise to treat you as I would like to be treated, and treat your time and money as precious. I look forward to hearing from you.

If the reader wants to know more, how can they connect with you?

If you want to put your retirement on cruise control, **email** me at returnonassets@hotmail.com and ask for the FREE report "How Long Will Your Retirement Last You?" Be sure to include "Free Report" in the subject line!

JACK HRADESKY, P.E., M.S.

Ceo & President
Tax-Fee Retirement Specialists

Email: **jhradesky@ca.rr.com**
Website: **www.taxfreeretirementspecialists.com**
Call: **(424) 228-4431**

My business's mission is to provide strategies and products to achieve retirement goals, meaning the ultimate overarching goal is to be anxiety-free and have peace of mind during retirement. Below is a list of deliverables.

1. Create a guaranteed retirement income plan for life that provides for your Essential Living Financial Requirements (Housing, food, transportation, emergencies, medical).

2. Create a retirement income plan that provides for life for your Financial Lifestyle Requirements (Vacations and cruises).

3. Provide options to have increasing income for inflation income.

4. Achieve safety of your principal, as a result you never lose money in the stock market.

Strategies to achieve the above goals:

1. Reduces your retirement taxes to zero or to a bracket close to zero

2. Create tax free income for your lifetime

3. Establish appropriate amounts of liquid emergency money and reposition the excessive money of your Taxable Money Account to Tax-Free Money Account (Each person has their money in three possible accounts, Taxable, Deferred Tax and /or Tax-Free)

4. Harness the growth of your Deferred Tax Money Account and reposition the excessive funds to your Tax-Free Money account.

5. Increase the money in your Tax-Free Money Account and create tax-free income

6. Convert your IRAs/401(k)s to tax-free money without paying the taxes from your pocket and avoid paying taxes over a lifetime of approximately 60 % of the amount of qualified money (taxes are based on future earnings)

7. Provides contribution to charity strategies to convert your IRAs/401(k)s to a Roth IRA and receive more money back over 20 years than you contributed.

8. Provide strategies to convert your IRA/401(k)s to provide tax-free benefits for mitigating your biggest financial threat, chronic illness expenses.

9. Reduce your taxes to zero on Social Security. This is a function of balancing and reposition of your money in the appropriate buckets with the aim of paying zero taxes on your social security.

Provide a liquid, safe and yields averaging 7.2% to replace your savings accounts and money market accounts.

Describe the clients you work with and the types of situations they encounter before they come to you for your help.

My clients, as prospects, are those who do not have a retirement plan; they fear taxes will increase due to the national debt and they continue to function in the old paradigm of investing. They believe investing in a 401k is appropriate; i.e., investing 100% of their funds in the stock market; continue the long-term buy and sell strategy and be diversified only in stocks, mutual funds, and bonds.

Cautionary advice: Some prospects cannot be helped. If the prospects have advisors and CPAs who some have been friends for years then, they blindly follow their recommendations. Hence, they stay in the same investments with the same advisors and expect different results. Einstein calls this the Definition of Insanity.

If the prospect self-invests, they are usually not open to working with anyone except themselves. They can only trust themselves, and some can't even trust themselves.

In regard to risk, they live in a bubble where most of their money is at risk in the stock market and believe this is the place to be. Even though they say they want safety. In regard to fees, they are not knowledgeable of the high fees in their 401(k)s and mutual funds.

In regard to taxes, they usually have excessive money in their Taxable Account; they have excessive IRA and 401k funds in their Deferred Tax Account and usually no money in the Tax-Free Account. The excess in the Tax Deferred Account needs to be repositioned into the Tax-Free Account via Roth IRAs and special designed life insurance policies, where the insured is the primary beneficiary.

The above current conditions set them up for the perfect storm for high taxes for the rest of their lives. Some economists suggest 40% of their earnings will go to taxes over their lifetime.

Many prospects are not aware that they can stretch their money five to seven years if they do not pay taxes on their Social Security income over their retirement. They have not been educated by their CPAs regarding Provincial income and how to reduce it.

The prospect's investment bubbles (the value system they function in) range from an extreme of being 100% invested in stocks and mutual funds or the opposite extreme of having 100% of their money in savings accounts and money markets earning 1% or less. The former ignores the risk while the latter is consumed with fear of risk. The latter prospects believe banks are the safest place to invest even if they make little or no earnings. They are unaware of or not interested in their loss of buying power. Both groups accept taxes as a given and have done nothing to mitigate the issue.

These prospects have not taken steps to mitigate their greatest retirement risks:

1. Running out money

2. Losing money in the stock market.

3. Paying excessive taxes.

4. Living with inflation.

5. Experiencing catastrophic expenses due to needing chronic illness care.

What common obstacles prevent your prospects and clients from mitigating their retirement risks?

Intellectually, they believe they want guaranteed income, tax-free income and/or minimized taxes. However, typically they have done nothing about it because of five prevalent reasons:

1. They are not emotionally involved; they have not experienced or anticipated any pain relative to finances.

2. They fear moving their money, hence procrastinate, and procrastination is a decision. This creates loss opportunity situations.

3. They have error thinking that CPAs are knowledgeable professionals to consult regarding new and unique investments, therefore not realizing they may be receiving ill-advised advice, remain in the status quo and experience lost opportunities.

4. They believe other advisors will give them an honest assessment and are capable of giving accurate opinions, again they are receiving erroneous information and continuing to make the same investments with no improvement in performance.

5. They believe they can research a subject on their own. They research topics that are not even applicable to their situation or applications that not relevant. Sometimes they research topics that are years old and obsolete. As a consequence, they become overwhelmed and confused.

Let's address each obstacle.

1. If the prospect does not have pain, they will never
   enhance their financial situation. Emotional pain can be
   described as a fear of running out of money; loss of assets
   from stock market declines, having inadequate time
   required to recover from any losses; concerned that the
   sequence of returns will catastrophically impact their
   lifestyle if they decide to retire when the market is
   tanking or tanked; not keeping up with inflation therefore
   losing buying power and paying taxes that decrease the
   length of time that their money will last.

   How much taxes one pays is a choice. The average
   taxpayer in America pays 40% of their income over their
   lifetime in taxes, both willfully and unconsciously. The 40% is
   comprised of paying taxes on earnings, savings, what they
   spend and inheritance tax. They are not aware they can
   legally pay less taxes if they properly plan. Paying taxes today
   will save on paying taxes in the future. Once they become
   aware of new strategies, they sometimes are not willing to
   accept any new strategies. Some people cannot accept change
   in any form, even to their own detriment. Unless they are
   willing to be educated and accept change, they will never
   enhance their financial position.

2. Many prospects fear moving their money, and when this feeling is entrenched in their value system, they usually will not enhance their financial position. They are pathological savers and stuck in past paradigms because the strategies were once successful. (A paradigm is one's intellectual perception or belief of concepts, models, methods, or values). The problem is they are living with past paradigms which are not performing well in a world of new paradigms.

The prospects may have huge amounts of money in either the stock market or the bank. These prospects cannot make decisions to reposition their money in safe investments for fear of losing large gains or doing something that is different than they have done in the past. These people are creatures of habit and are not open-minded or ever think out of the box. Unless there is an acceptable intervention, these prospects will never enhance their financial position. They prefer to commit slow financial erosion.

3. Many prospects erroneously believe CPAs are knowledgeable in all types of investments and even worse, in new strategies and investment vehicles. The truth is that CPAs have 100,000 pages of IRS codes, regulations, rules, and case histories to deal with, and these

documents change monthly. This is a career in itself, just like a doctor, engineer, or attorney. How in the world can a CPA be knowledgeable in multitudes of investment vehicles which change rapidly? To be an expert in these strategies requires the same dedication as CPAs need in their profession. It is not reasonable for a CPA to be knowledgeable of all investment vehicles. Occasionally a CPA will be knowledgeable, but it is because they own the product.

"CPAs are tax preparers/historians and not tax strategists," per Ed Slott, CPA who the Wall Street Journal calls "America's Expert in IRAs." He describes himself as a recovering CPA. He also said, "The CPA primary function is to look at the past for historical tax data and not in the future." The CPAs mantra '3 Ds'. Delay, defer and deduct. The tax strategist focuses on the future." CPAs are more entrenched in past paradigms than the average person. However, there always are exceptions.

Very few are open-minded as they do not have the time. It is unreasonable for CPAs to have the time be aware of the new tax strategies in life insurance let alone be knowledgeable in the product. There are exceptions, however. I have four CPA clients as of this writing and have met one other who owns the latest strategies in living benefit life insurance.

Their expectations is to achieve tax-free income and avoid significant taxes over his lifetime.

Now there is a small percentage of CPAs who actually sell the same products or who work with advisors like myself. When you consult them, they will try to sell you. The moral of the story is that if the CPA does not know the strategy or product, he/she will not recommend it. The prospect has to be knowledgeable and have the wisdom to be independent of the CPA opinion. What they do not know, is more important than what they know.

4. When prospects hear new strategies, they immediately ask their financial advisors regarding the strategies. They wonder why their financial advisor never spoke to them about the subjects. The reason their financial advisor never addressed them is one of three reasons: (a) they do not know how to do it; (b) they do not want you to know; or (c) if they heard of it, they do not have any experience in implementing it. I do not know which is worse.

Prospects do not realize that the advisor would never recommend anything he/she does not sell because it will reduce their income.

5. Some prospects believe they can research the subject on their own. This is serious error thinking. The layman does not know what they do not know. They do not know the right sources to evaluate. They do not know which sources are reliable and which are not. Even if they did know, they do not have the criteria to evaluate the information.

The internet is a common source of information. However, there is accurate information and erroneous information. Some of the erroneous information is outdated by as much as 10 years. Other information is intentionally biased with self-serving purposes of the writer. Some of the writers are not even qualified or licensed to speak about a subject.

What is needed to help these prospects is that they recognize the limitations in doing their own research and be coachable regarding what to research, specifically textbooks, videos, and third-party resources. Everyone needs a coach or Sherpa who they can trust,

Share examples of how you would help your prospects to successfully overcome the common barriers that prevent them from achieving their retirement goals.

Obstacle #1. The prospect is not emotionally involved.

The probable source of this condition is that the prospect has experienced no pain, or they do not recognize they have a future problem.

The solution to helping these prospects is to provide them a retirement income plan of the status quo which points out when they will run out of money relative to their lifestyle. They have to have the wisdom to understand it and understand the impact. Otherwise, you can lead the horse to water, but you cannot make him drink.

Obstacle #2. The prospect fears moving their money, hence procrastinates.

The probable source of this condition is that the prospect has had experiences of losing money, has no confidence they can make a right decision or do not recognize they may have a future problem. One prospect recently told me that she regrets listening to her brothers as the product that she if not buy, earned 12 and 13% tax-free for the last two years.

The solution to help these prospects is through education with books, videos, and third-party sources. However, the prospects must be willing to invest the time and be able to learn. Otherwise, you can lead a horse to water, but cannot make him drink. Hence the prospect loses.

Obstacle #3. The prospect erroneously believes all CPAs are knowledgeable regarding all investments, hence receive inaccurate information, obsolete information, and opinions dealing with past paradigms. Hence, the information is ill-advised, and the prospect remains in the status quo.

The probable source of this condition is that the prospect has had a successful experience in asking their CPA regarding common investments. However, when they consult the CPA on new and specialized strategies, the typical CPA has not heard of them. The CPA either inaccurately understands the strategies from the prospect or has outdated information or have no basis to make an opinion, so they automatically give a negative recommendation. Many times, the prospect cannot articulate the strategy to their CPA. The negative recommendation is always a safe recommendation.

The solution to help these prospects is to educate them along with their CPA. However, the CPA must be willing to invest the time and be willing to learn. If the CPA is not willing, the prospect must be willing to invest the time themselves and be willing to learn the concepts and be knowledgeable to make the decisions themselves. This will provide them the wisdom to not use the CPAs opinion.

Obstacle #4. The prospect believes other advisors will give them an honest assessment, hence continue to do the same with no improvement.

The probable source of this condition is that the prospect has had successful experience interfacing with their financial advisor regarding investments. However, when they consult their financial advisor on specialized strategies which change as fast as technology, the typical advisor has not heard of them. If they have heard of them, they either interpret them inaccurately or only have knowledge of historical strategies.

The only solution to help these prospects is to have them consult with their financial advisor in order to provide them a fix-it plan and when the advisor cannot, hope the prospect has the wisdom of understanding their advisor's motivation and have the courage to ignore them. The prospect must be willing to invest the time and be willing to learn, to have the wisdom to ignore the financial advisor's opinion and be knowledgeable in order to make the decisions themselves.

Obstacle #5. The prospect believes they can research a subject on their own and discovers they are overwhelmed and confused by all the information.

The probable source of this condition is that the prospect has had successful experience in researching their own investments. Typical investments are stocks, mutual funds, and bonds. There is much accurate information on these subjects.

However. When they try to research specialized strategies, i.e., converting IRAs and 401(k) to tax-free income strategies, it is a different ballgame. The products change so fast, one has to specialize in the investment.

Some people want to research a subject that may not even be applicable to them. One cannot know what vehicle is applicable or not until the financial analysis is conducted by a professional planner. This analysis is part of the process of developing a retirement plan. The retirement plan dictates the types of investment vehicles and how they need to be customized.

The solution to helping these people is to provide them third with third-party sources, textbooks, videos, white papers and education regarding the pros and cons of how the products work. However, the prospect must be willing to invest the time and be willing to learn, have the wisdom to not use their own sources and be knowledgeable to make their own decisions.

Obstacle #6. The prospect has been wired throughout their lifetime to make short-term investments, and a long-term commitment of their money is a new paradigm.

The probable source of this condition is that the prospect has had successful experiences in investing for the short term. However, now they want income for life and guaranteed income. This is a conflict in their value system. What has been working successfully in the past, but not working today? The difference is a conflict between what they want and what they are doing.

The solution to helping these people is for them to analyze and prioritize each item of conflict. Will their money when liquid, not earning anything and safely provide for their needs? As for example, do they want a Fixed Indexed annuity that will provide guaranteed income for life and increase income with the stock market increases be willing to give up the liquidity? This is a simple 'yes' or 'no' answer.

What are 2-3 popular myths/misconceptions that the people you serve may have about achieving their desired outcome?

The Old Paradigm relative to retirement. Pre-retirees are told:

1. *You will be in a lower tax bracket.* The truth is you will be in a lower tax bracket only if you did not save any qualified money. If you saved money as IRA or 401(k)s, all qualified money is taxed as ordinary income upon distribution. Hence you will be in an equal tax bracket if you maintain your level of income.

2. You will be living on less income in retirement. The truth is I have not experienced anyone who wants to live on less money in retirement.

3. Tax-deferred investments are the most effective method to build wealth for retirement. The truth is that other vehicles can be safer, make comparable yields and are tax-free in distribution.

4. You pay taxes according to the tax code per your CPA's advice. The truth is that most CPAs and financial advisors are not aware of the strategies in addition to Roth IRAs which can reduce your taxes to zero or a bracket close to

zero. In addition, CPAs look at the past when your needs are for a tax strategist that looks to the future.

You will experience relative to the New Paradigm to retirement:

1. Your tax bracket may be higher in the future than today. The truth is if you have large amounts of money in IRAs or 401(k)s, your distributions will be taxed as ordinary income. You will have fewer deductions. Taxes have a high likelihood of increasing due to the national debt.

2. You may need as much income in your retirement as you did during your working years. The truth is this is the common goal of retirees.

3. Tax-deferred investments like 401(k)s should be contributed to only when there are matching funds. The truth is that anything more to match funds is a misallocation of your money.

4. You may lose your greatest deductions in your retirement years. The truth is your home will be paid off, your children left home, and you will not be having 401(k) contribution deductions.

5. Our country's fiscal challenges may force higher tax rates. The truth is there will be a date in the near future where

the 19.5 trillion dollars will be required to be paid back. Interest rates which are now 2.2% sometime in the future be required to return to 5% interest rate as it was in 2000.

6. Positioning yourself to not pay taxes on your Social Security income will extend the life of your assets five to seven years. Has your CPA discussed provincial income with you? This is a prerequisite for tax-free planning. The truth can be discovered by doing the math.

7. Accumulating assets in accounts that are tax deferred and have tax-free distributions will be commonplace. The truth is that the use of IRS Code 7702 will create tax-free income.

The Old Paradigm relative to chronic illnesses.

1. Medical insurance will pay for long-term care expenses. The truth is Medi-Cal insurance will pay for the first 21 days in California. If you are improving, Medi-Cal will increase payments to 100 days. If you are not improving, you are asked to leave the hospital

2. Assets can be gifted away in order to qualify for Medi-Cal. The truth is that there is a five-year look back wherein your heirs will be responsible for your expenses. There is a

risk if your heirs divorce that you will lose a portion of your assets.

3. Your children will take care of aging parents. The truth is if your children have families and/or a successful career, they will not have time to take care of you.

4. You believe you will not need any chronic illness service because you are healthy now. The probability that any person at the age of 65 needing some form of Long Term Care is 70%. This happened to my dad, and he spent $650,000 in today's dollars.

5. There are only three ways to mitigate long-term care risks. One is to self-insure; two is to rely on other family members; and three is to buy expensive long-term care insurance. The truth is one has to have accounts with up to a million dollars and a written plan which identifies which accounts to liquidate in sequence and which accounts the taxes are sourced from. Having family members take care of you is really punishing them and the probability the caregivers die before the care receiver is 70%.

The New Paradigm relative to chronic illness in California one will experience is:

1. Basic Home care will cost $5000 a month plus nurses, etc. Basic Assisted living will cost $7,000 a month, and Nursing Home Care can cost up to $13,000 a month depending on the area.

2. Medi-Cal does not pay for long-term care unless you are broke and have no money.

3. Medi-Cal only steps in when you have a stroke

4. Chronic illness care can destroy a lifetime of savings before it reaches the next generation. It can punish your spouse if you do not have coverage.

5. Children are often incapable or resist taking on long-term care duties

6. Expensive long-term care insurance is no longer the only way to safeguard against a long-term care event.

7. Qualified money (IRA, 401(k), 403(b), SEP, etc. can be used to buy long-term care coverage, a death benefit if you do not use it, a return of premium if you want your money returned at any time.

What pitfalls or mistakes should the reader be mindful of?

There are three pitfalls in the distribution of your assets:

Pitfall #1. Withdrawing money too quickly; Pitfall #2. Liquidating your assets in the wrong order; and Pitfall #3. Getting the wrong sequence of returns on your investments during the distribution phase.

Pitfall #1. Withdrawing money too quickly. Two questions you need to ask yourself: "How long do you plan on living in retirement?" or "What is your life expectancy?"

The younger you are at retirement, the less you should withdraw. If you retire at 70, you can withdraw 6 to 7 %. If you retire at 62, that number reduces to 2 to 3%. The real issue is when do you plan to retire?

William Bengen's theory predicted an average rate of return of 8% for stocks and 6.6% for bonds. Today, the bond average is 2.4%. Stocks are projected to be lower than the past. In today's environment, a 4% withdrawal rate may be too aggressive.

If you are invested in a 100% bond portfolio with a 4% withdrawal rate, he predicts you have a 35% chance your money will last 30 years.

If you are invested in 75% stocks and 25% bonds with a 4% withdrawal rate, he predicts there is a 100% chance your money will last 30 years.

If you are withdrawing at a 6 % rate, with 100% bonds, he predicts you have an 11% chance of lasting 30 years.

If you are withdrawing at a 6 % rate, with 75% stocks and 25% bonds, he predicts you have a 60% chance of lasting 30 years.

Other variables impacting withdrawal rates are tax rates, Social Security income, pensions, part-time work, and order of liquidation.

Pitfall #2. The order of liquidation. This is the sequence or order you spend down your money. Spending down assets in the wrong sequence or order can dramatically affect how long your retirement funds will last.

There are three types of retirement assets. A Taxable Bucket, A Tax Deferred Bucket, and a Tax-Free Bucket. The use of financial planning software will assist in determining which bucket to liquidate first. If you randomly withdraw your money, a case study shows you can run out of money at age 93. However, if you use computer algorithms, your retirement funds can stretch to age 100. This is the ultimate solution.

A general rule is to convert your IRAs and 401(k)s to a Roth if the math works out, or convert your IRA and 401(k) to tax-free income, and then you want to spend down your remaining IRA and 401(k)s first so when taxes increase, it will have a minimum impact. Another rule is to position your Roths and IRA/401(k)s in a Principal Protection Program, (Fixed Indexed Annuities) and in an investment which increases the income annually and is tax-free. The last money you spend should be your after-tax money.

Pitfall #3. The sequence of Returns. The sequence of returns is the order of your investment returns. As you know, the stock market is like a rollercoaster. It goes up, and it goes down. If the market goes down in pre-retirement years, you experience negative returns in your early years of retirement. The impact can be significant and reduce your assets. If negative returns occur later in retirement, the impact will be minimal.

If you experience negative returns in your early years of retirement while you are taking withdrawals, the impact can be catastrophic and erode all your assets. The chances of this occurring are the luck of the draw.

However, there is a potential solution. You reallocate a portion of your retirement savings to a Principal Protection Program, which is Fixed Indexed Annuities. This protects your assets from the risk of negative returns while withdrawing income during the early retirement years. This empowers you to benefit from periods of high returns in later retirement years.

Retirement Distribution Pitfall #1: Withdrawing money too soon.

By withdrawing too much too soon, you may outlive your assets

Solution: Never withdraw more than 4% of your assets and perhaps less.

Retirement Distribution Pitfall #2: Order of Liquidation.

By liquidating your assets in the wrong order, you may unknowingly deplete your retirement assets.

Solution: Use a computer software that determines the appropriate order of liquidation.

Retirement Distribution Pitfall #3: Sequence of Return Risk.

If you experience negative returns in early retirement years while taking withdrawals, your portfolio may never recover.

Solution: Allocate a portion of your retirement funds to a Principal Protection Program (Fixed Indexed Annuities).

What common fears hold your prospects and clients back from even trying to achieve their retirement goals?

Most laypeople, CPAs and financial advisor's perception of life insurance is that it is exclusively limited to death benefits. When they hear the words life insurance, it is a turn-off. If they are single, they believe they do not need it, and if married, many do not want to leave anything to their children. Both are false assumptions.

The truth is that living benefit life insurance is 180 degrees from their perception. The life insurance we are discussing is living benefits for the insured, not their heirs. This is a paradigm shift in their thinking, and some people cannot handle it. They claim it is counter-intuitive. This is truly a New Paradigm.

An analogy to the life insurance is like looking at a zebra and a horse. Their silhouette appears the same, however, the difference between the two is huge. The horse has significantly more utility than a zebra, and the zebra has stripes, and the horse does not.

The difference between a death benefit insurance policy and living benefit insurance policy is likewise huge. The insured is the beneficiary of a living benefit policy. The death benefit insurance policy has a high cost of insurance and leaves a large death benefit of tax-free money to one's heirs. The living benefit insurance policy has a low cost of insurance and provides significant tax-free income to the insured and a small death benefit to the heirs. It may also provide disability insurance and chronic illnesses insurance. The death benefit policy requires non-qualified money (after tax money) premiums. The living benefit policy can be funded indirectly using qualified as well as non-qualified money premiums depending upon the design of the policy.

The living benefit insurance policy can be used to convert IRAs and 401(k)s to tax-free income due to a special design. Living benefit life insurance is essential to utilize if your goals are to pay zero taxes in retirement or in a bracket close to zero.

The question always comes up, "Why have I not heard of this before?" There are several answers. Until recently this product has been limited to the top 1% of taxpayers. These are individuals whose AGI is $369,000 and higher. This translates to only a select few CPAs, financial advisors and insurance agents who have experience in the strategy. Since it takes a lot of knowledge to be familiar with the strategies, only the ones involved are competent in the strategy because they have taken the training and have experience. These policies require knowledge like a Ph.D. as compared to a Bachelor's Degree.

The other reasons are that your financial advisors, agents, and CPAs do not know about it, or do not want you to know about it or they cannot sell it to you. Hence they will lose income, or if they have heard about it, they have no experience in implementing it. I am not sure which is worse.

It is common when an insurance agent who does not sell this type of product will be asked about it, they will have a negative response. What they do not know, they just do not know. But one thing for sure. If they do know about it, they will try to sell you on their product. The agents may even try to sell you the same product, even if they have never sold one before. This has happened several times and with CPAs as well. I am always amazed why someone would ask their agents for an opinion on a product and eventually buy it from them when the agent failed to offer it to them previously.

When you are asking an insurance agent, financial advisor, or CPA for their opinion, ask if they have a license to sell it, how much training they have taken and how many policies have they implemented. Otherwise, you are asking someone who is not qualified to give you a qualified opinion.

My purpose is to make these strategies available to everyone who can benefit and afford them.

The other issue which surfaces is that many laypeople as well as brokers, financial advisors and CPAs are that they just do not trust insurance companies. Most will have some negative experience with an auto insurance or property casualty company. None can articulate problems, such as not paying premiums and expecting benefits, as their issues.

The insurance industry for life insurance and annuities is highly regulated by the states. The independent rating agencies rate the insurance carriers based on their claim paying records and the amount of surplus assets they have relative to liabilities. I like work with A+ rated companies. The ratings of insurance companies are based on their history of paying claims and are required to have surplus assets so they can guarantee their liabilities and their policyholders benefit,

A frequently asked question is, "What happens if the insurance company goes bankrupt?" The last insurance company to go bankrupt was Executive Life in 1996. Not one company has gone bankrupt since then. However, hundreds of banks have gone bankrupt since then.

The insurance industry for life insurance and annuities is monitored and regulated by state insurance departments. One of their primary objectives is to protect policyholders from the risk of a company in financial distress.

The first thing is that another insurance company always buys out the assets if one would go bankrupt. The buyer continues the contracts. I have two clients who have received all their premiums back from Executive Life and a third who received a better annuity than I can provide today from the carrier who purchased Executive Life.

The State Guaranty Association is organized to protect claimant's policyholders, annuitants, and insolvent insurers by providing them funds for payments of claims.

The details of how it works and responsibilities and limits of the guarantees are on the following website:

www.nolhga.com

It sounds obvious, but why would the people you serve want to be anxiety-free and have peace of mind in their retirement years?

Let's address each of the deliverables.

1. Create a retirement income plan that provides guaranteed income for life for your Essential Living Financial Requirements, i.e., expenses for home, food, medical, transportation, and entertainment.

   - *Personal Benefit:* Your income is guaranteed to meet your Essential Living Requirement.

   - *Emotional Benefit:* **You are anxiety-free and have Peace of Mind.**

2. Create a retirement income plan that provides variable income for life for your Lifestyle Financial Requirements

   - *Personal Benefit:* Funds are generated to provide for vacations, cruises, and cars for your pleasure

   - *Emotional Benefit:* **You are anxiety-free and have Peace of Mind.**

3. Provide options to prospects for increasing income to keep up with inflation or level income.

- *Personal Benefit:* Your income keeps up with inflation

- *Emotional Benefit:* **You are anxiety-free and have Peace of Mind.**

4. Achieve safety of the client's principal

- *Personal Benefit:* You never worry or experience the loss of principal.

- *Emotional Benefit:* **You are Anxiety-free and have Peace of Mind.**

5. Reduces the prospect's retirement taxes to zero or to a bracket close to zero.

- *Personal Benefit:* You significantly stretch your money and leave more money for your heirs. You legally fulfill your tax responsibility.

- *Emotional Benefit:* **You are anxiety-free and have Peace of Mind.**

6. Create tax-free income for life.

- *Personal Benefit:* You significantly stretch your money and leave more money for your heirs. You legally fulfill your tax responsibility.

- *Emotional Benefit*: **You are anxiety-free and have Peace of Mind.**

7. Reposition the prospect's excessive money from their Taxable Bucket to achieve appropriate emergency levels.

   - *Personal Benefit*: You significantly stretch your money and leave more money for your heirs. You legally fulfill your tax responsibility.

   - *Emotional Benefit*: **You are anxiety-free and have Peace of Mind.**

8. Harness the growth of your Deferred Tax Bucket and reposition the excess funds to your Tax-Free Bucket.

   - *Personal Benefit*: You significantly stretch your money and leave more money for your heirs. You legally fulfill your tax responsibility.

   - *Emotional Benefit*: **You are anxiety-free and have Peace of Mind.**

9. Increase the money in your Tax-Free Bucket.

   - *Personal Benefit*: You significantly stretch your money and leave more money for your heirs. You legally fulfill your tax responsibility.

- *Emotional Benefit*: **You are anxiety-free and have Peace of Mind.**

10. Convert IRAs/401(k)s to tax-free money without paying the taxes out-of-pocket and avoid paying taxes over a lifetime of 60% of the amount of qualified money, The forecasted taxes is based on the estimated earnings your IRA/401(k) would create taxes over your lifetime.

    - *Personal Benefit*: You significantly stretch your money and leave more money for your heirs. You legally fulfill your tax responsibility.

    - *Emotional Benefit*: **You are anxiety-free and have Peace of Mind.**

11. Provides strategies for contribution to charity to convert IRAs/401(k)s to a Roth IRA and receive more money back over 20 years than contributed and receive handsome tax deductions.

    - *Personal Benefit*: You significantly stretch your money and leave more money for your heirs. You legally fulfill your tax responsibility.

    - *Emotional Benefit*: **You are anxiety-free and have Peace of Mind.**

12. Provide strategies to convert IRA/401(k)s to provide tax-free benefits for mitigating your biggest financial threat.... chronic illness expenses.

- *Personal Benefit*: You will not reduce the lifestyle of your spouse, not spend down your assets and leave more money for your heirs.

- *Emotional Benefit*: **You are anxiety-free and have Peace of Mind.**

13. Reduce your taxes on Social Security. This is a function of balancing and reposition of your money in the appropriate buckets with the aim of paying zero taxes on Social Security.

- *Personal Benefit*: You significantly stretch your money and leave more money for your heirs. You legally fulfill your tax responsibility.

- *Emotional Benefit*: **You are anxiety-free and have Peace of Mind.**

14. Provide a liquid and safe vehicle which yields averaging 7.2% to replace savings accounts and money market accounts and be as liquid.

- *Personal Benefit*: You significantly stretch your money and leave more money for your heirs. You legally fulfill your tax responsibility.

- *Emotional Benefit*: **You are anxiety-free and have Peace of Mind.**

What got you started in the financial services field?

My career has three segments.

Education

- Industrial Engineer at the University of Pittsburgh

- Master in Statistics at Rochester Institute of Technology.

- Professional Engineer, State of California

First career

- Working for General Motors, Eastman Kodak, Xerox, American Hospital Supply, and Johnson and Johnson. Started as an engineer and foreman and promoted to Vice President of Manufacturing.

Second career

CEO/President, founded the National Summit Group, a consulting and training firm that focused on growth, profits via strategic planning and quality dominance for manufacturing and administrative companies.

Transition

Experience an epiphany long before entering the financial services. In 1997, when NAFTA was passed in Congress, predicted the US would have 5 million people out of work by mid-2000s. Unfortunately, my firm, as well as all my competition, were impacted as millions of manufacturing jobs were outsourced. Never thought that I would be a victim of NAFTA's poor decision.

When my firm was impacted, had to decide what I wanted to do. Was attracted to helping individuals, similar as I did with corporations. Started to specialize in being unique in learning various strategies on reducing taxes, using arbitrage like banks and having a guaranteed income.

During the seventies and eighties, the only retirement education that was available was from stock brokers. After experiencing 1987 stocks fall, in my opinion, the reason they are called 'brokers' was because they made "you broke."

Third career

When starting meeting with prospects, discovered that many people had been ill-advised by stock brokers, CPAs, and security advisors with all kinds of professional designations. It blew me away how many of them had antiquated biases and did not use all the options available. Today, nothing has changed. It does not matter how many professional designations one has because the designations do not reflect product knowledge. It amazes me if you asked the same question to five stockbrokers, five CPAs, and five security advisors, you could get 15 different answers.

Discovered many of these advisors were excellent in their jobs, but many do not have the interest nor time to invest in becoming retirement specialists or tax-free retirement specialists along with their full-time professional occupation. They just do not have the time to attain the advanced knowledge of insurance products and keep current with the ongoing changes. It is a full-time job.

Started on my quest to be extremely versed and educated in retirement planning, specializing in tax-free strategies for guaranteed income, tax-free income and paying zero taxes or be in a bracket closer to zero than you are today. Now preparing to become licensed as an investment advisor. While I have always put my client's interest first, even with the new license, there will be no different behavior than I have already been practicing for years.

What are your final thoughts for the reader who wants to manage their finances, never run out of money during retirement and have total peace of mind?

My final thoughts are for someone who desires to be anxiety-free retirement resulting in peace of mind.

One has to commit to:

1. Have a retirement plan and make an effort to have it happen.

2. Meet three to four times on successive weeks to achieve the desired goal.

Understand when you run out of money in the 'status quo' plan.

Identify your realistic Financial Essential Living Requirements and Lifestyle Requirements Plan.

Identify your goals and visions during retirement.

Identify your financial resources.

3. Review the initial plan and tweak it.

4. Become educated on the various strategies and products.

Identify what you like and do not like and proceed with the process.

Be able to make a decision to go forward or terminate in each section.

If the reader wants to know more, how can they connect with you?

They can reach me via email: jhradesky@ca.rr.com

Visit: www.taxfreeretirementspecialists.com

Call: (424) 228-4431

ABOUT THE AUTHOR

Mark Imperial is a Best Selling Author, Syndicated Business Columnist, Syndicated Radio Host, and internationally recognized Stage, Screen, and Radio Host of numerous business shows spotlighting leading experts, entrepreneurs, and business celebrities.

His passion is discovering noteworthy business owners, professionals, experts, and leaders who do great work, and sharing their stories and secrets to their success with the world on his syndicated radio program titled "Remarkable Radio".

Mark is also the media marketing strategist and voice for some of the world's most famous brands. You can hear his voice over the airwaves weekly on Chicago radio and worldwide on iHeart Radio.

Mark is a Karate black belt, teaches kickboxing, loves Thai food, House Music, and his favorite TV show is infomercials.

Learn more:

www.MarkImperial.com

www.ImperialAction.com

www.RemarkableRadioShow.com

www.ingramcontent.com/pod-product-compliance
Lightning Source LLC
Chambersburg PA
CBHW060002100426
42740CB00010B/1367